INTEGRITY....

Adherence to moral and ethical principles; soundness of moral character; honesty.

Source: Webster's Encyclopedic Unabridged Dictionary.

"Each of us decides for our self our own degree of participation."

Joe

OTHER BOOKS BY JOE GWERDER

Listen Without Your Ears: The Road Ahead

Listen Out Loud: Broaden Your Horizon

20/20 Listening: Clarity

Learn More At:

www.solarintegrity.net
www.thelistenbooks.com
www.thelistenbooks.net
www.thelistenbooks.org

SoLAR
INTEGRITY

JOE GWERDER

ARCHWAY
PUBLISHING

Archway Publishing books may be ordered through booksellers or by contacting:

Archway Publishing
1663 Liberty Drive
Bloomington, IN 47403
www.archwaypublishing.com
1-(888)-242-5904

ISBN: 978-1-4808-1114-0 (sc)
ISBN: 978-1-4808-1116-4 (hc)
ISBN: 978-1-4808-1115-7 (e)

Library of Congress Control Number: 2014916572

Printed in the United States of America.

Archway Publishing rev. date: 10/6/2014

DEDICATION

This book is dedicated to an attempt to ensure the long-term continued use of solar components in the private sector. A tremendous benefit can be realized by all those who obtain these products via qualified and ethical avenues. In the near future significant issues will arise that will pose a threat to the popularity of this industry. It should be known that in nearly every case these coming harsh judgments will have originated with the people involved and not due to a dissatisfaction of equipment performance. As we will unveil throughout this book, an enormous amount of greed, incompetence and arrogance are prevalent in today's solar industry. I am absolutely convinced that in a few short years a much different public opinion will materialize revealing our current injustices. I am dedicating this book to my belief in the use of the equipment.

Joe

Editorial Note from the Author

The content in this book, as with all of my books, was written with a significant amount of "listening" to my intuition. I wrote it as I felt it. In doing so, there are instances where standard protocols of punctuation and/or grammar are compromised. With authenticity and integrity as my priority, I do not involve any professional editing. Understanding my priorities, Archway Publishing Company has graciously allowed any punctuation and/or grammar variances. It should be known, the writing style is completely my own and has remained at my request.

Joe

TABLE OF CONTENTS

ACKNOWLEDGEMENTS

To be completely honest, I must reveal that the experiences and knowledge I have gained, which has guided me throughout the content of this book, was founded with a significant amount of hardship. Were it left to only positive experiences within my journey of the solar industry, I do not believe this book would have materialized. It is ironic that an involvement of such a large amount of negative exposures is directly responsible for a book that has such positive potential. It is for this reason that I wish to openly acknowledge all those people and practices that I have struggled with tremendously. Although these many occurrences have had specific traumatic effects on me personally during certain timeframes, they have provided an overall enormous amount of purpose for the truths and awareness's revealed in these pages. It does seem odd to me that an author would acknowledge the very things that have caused him so much anguish. Even so, I am doing just that. Because for me, the creation of this book greatly outweighs any short-term personal struggle.

Joe

SPECIAL ACKNOWLEDGEMENTS

To read all of my books will show a particular redundancy that I am extremely happy to continue repeating. The dedication, talents, and sincerity of my Office Manager only continue to expand. She is a very integral part of the physical production of these books. She only brings 100% effort to her tasks. Thank you Christie!

I would also like to extend my gratitude to Chris Kapsalis. Chris is a local artist that provided the car sketch in Chapter 4. He very accurately transformed my description into that drawing.

INTRODUCTION

The messages in this book are very important! In fact, I believe that the solar industry in the U.S. is on very thin ice. As I write this, it is mid-2014. Most of what I will expose and express to you in these pages will come as news you have not heard before. Some of you will believe every word. Others will agree with certain aspects and not wish to accept others. And there will also be those among you who will discount nearly all of this content. Your own level of acceptance or denial is completely up to you. I will say though that I have made up nothing. What is revealed within my personal stories is without exaggeration. If I am expressing opinion, I will openly disclose this.

I will also suggest that if you are currently involved in the solar industry, your individual exposures thus far have created your model of what this industry stands for and where it is potentially headed. The very same is true for me also. However, as we will come to realize, my personal exposures have been very diversified and unique. There is somewhat of a "perfect storm" prevalent in the current solar industry that is potentially very volatile in my opinion. Actually, I believe we are past a point of preventing damaging issues in our near future. It is my purpose to expose what I truly believe are the main threats to the popularity and acceptance of these products in an attempt to avoid a complete collapse. This may sound a bit extreme at this point in time, but I expect by the conclusion of this book you will at least have some questions toward the future of how the solar business in America will look in the next decade.

Please allow me to be perfectly clear; no one believes in the benefit of solar products more than I do. Likewise, few approach the promotion of these products like I do (at least not currently). There is an old saying: "Look to see which way the masses are going, then go in the opposite direction". This may not be absolutely true in every case, but with regard to the current approach by most who sell and install solar products, I believe this is the best advice I could suggest.

Joe

DEFINITION

I have found that few people actually understand the basic function of solar (photovoltaics). Let's take a minute here to outline how these products perform. I believe that most of you will associate the word "solar" with the sun. In fact, this is probably the only way you have heard of this industry referred to until now. "Solar" is indeed a direct reference to the sun, but what does "photovoltaic" mean? Typically called "P.V.", photovoltaic is the process of creating voltage (electrical pressure) from light. "Photo", from the word "photology" means the "science of light". "Voltaic", from the word "voltaism" means "electricity produced by chemical action". In short, this process makes electricity from light. I'll bet that this comes as a surprise to many of you. I can say that by far, most people I encounter assume the value is found in the heat from the sun. This is an understandable assumption given the fact that we place the solar modules in direct sun intentionally.

The solar modules are typically referred to as panels. These are the large, flat, dark colored items that are usually seen on a roof or ground frame of some sort. The function of the modules is to gather light from the sun which causes the chemical reaction in a silicon based cell to become active. A typical solar module will have a grouping of 60 or 72 cells wired in a particular way to increase or multiply the individual voltage created in each cell. With this, each module is given a power rating. In

2007, when I first became involved in this industry, the module power ratings were generally 150-175 watts. As I write this now in 2014, a standard solar module will have a rating between 240-300 watts. In future chapters, I will expand on a few of the most common electrical terms and their function in order to give you a basic understanding of how this all works. For now though, you can easily realize that in the past seven years solar modules have dramatically increased in strength.

I would like to return briefly to the concept of light and heat. I routinely say to my clients that a clear, cool day is the prime circumstance for P.V. (photovoltaic) activity. The fact that here in the U.S. we generate more solar energy on any given clear summer day versus a clear winter day has everything to do with total quantity of sunlight hours in the day. The industry standard for testing and assigning a module its particular power rating is done at 77 degrees Fahrenheit. So basically speaking, on days warmer than 77 the modules will lose a little of their capacity based on their rating and likewise they will gain a little on days cooler than 77 (to a point). The ratio of power loss on hot days is worth less than the amount of light exposure gained with longer summer days. Therefore, a greater total amount of power is generated with long hot days than with short cool days. With this understanding, we can realize why installers are looking for non-shaded locations and the most direct angle toward the sun as possible.

By far the most applied scenario is a "grid-tied" or "grid-interactive" system. As the name implies, the current utility or grid power that is present at the location remains fully functional and engaged. A properly installed P.V. system is connected by various methods that we will discuss later. The new arrangement becomes one of coexistence between the P.V. system and the utility. The primary purpose of the solar equipment is to produce some or all of the power for the electrical "load" demands for a particular location. Contrary to popular belief, a standard P.V. system does not provide electrical power during utility outages. There are however, extra steps that can be taken to provide the necessary equipment that will supply power during such utility outages. The general purpose of a standard P.V. system in conjunction with utility power is to return the costs of the utility power to the consumer by generating and providing or replacing power as the conditions allow. Much like a bank account, the utility meter will record and keep track of the net difference between your power withdrawals and deposits as time passes.

By definition, once any location engages a solar P.V. system to the electrical load demands and/or to the coexisting utility grid, that location is now referred to as a "generating facility or location". As the above definition implies, as a consumer of electricity who typically purchases the power from the local utility, one now has the ability to, either partially or completely, produce their own power for consumption and/or replacement toward the utility. An option now exists for the consumer that did not exist before in most cases. Although rarely used in most populated areas, a fully independent solar power system can be configured to provide the electrical needs of most residences and even some smaller commercial settings providing the conditions of the location accommodate enough sunlight and area. If utility power is readily available and in close proximity to the location of the desired power needs, a completely independent P.V. system is typically not applied for cost reasons.

What it really comes down to is the individual priorities of the consumer. Mechanically speaking, a system can be very flexible and accommodate a wide variety of needs and desires.

CHAPTER 1

Getting Started

It is late 2007. I walked into my office and sat down across from my office manager. I met Marlene a few years sooner somewhat by "accident". My company was doing a construction job in a cul-de-sac in Woodland, California. One day a very nice elderly woman, who lived a few houses down, walked up to me and asked if she could throw a few items in my trailer that had the tear-out materials from our project in it. She wanted to discard these items but did not have the means to haul them herself. I told her I would be more than happy to help. I sent a couple of my employees with her to gather her unwanted items. When all of the unwanted items were removed from her house she came back and asked to pay me. I refused and said that it was really no problem. She again attempted payment but I was not going to take any money from her. Finally she very appreciatively agreed and walked back across the street. I thought that this was the end of it and also I was really quite happy to have helped her. However, this was not so.

The next morning her daughter walked up to me from the same house and introduced herself. Her name was Marlene and her mother lived with her. She was also very grateful for our previous assistance. Marlene then attempted reimbursement but as with her mom I declined. Not taking no for an answer, she asked if she could return the favor with her skills in office work. Before long, I was employing her on a part-time basis during her free time. She set up a simple Tupperware container on her porch where we could exchange papers she typed for me etc. Not having a personal desire for very much office work myself, I was very happy to obtain her skills. My company was quite busy with construction projects and as time passed she was ready for a change from her other job, so we discussed a position with my company on a full-time basis. Approximately 1½ years after her mom walked across the street, I opened an office on Main Street in Woodland and Marlene managed it.

Now several years later, it is late 2007, and the construction business is fading fast. The housing boom that had been going crazy for a few years was rapidly declining. As I sat across from Marlene that day in our office, I simply said to her, "I think we should look into solar". The past year or so had been tough for us. Trying to keep as many of my employees as I could, I would create unnecessary work at times to provide them with a paycheck. This depleted any surplus of funds we had quickly. So now I was very worried. Responding to my "solar" statement, Marlene simply said, "Oh, ok". For me personally, the electrical portion of building a house was always my favorite. Although I would do nearly all of the different aspects of construction with my own crew, when it came time for the wiring I would be right there doing it myself. I really liked it, I was good at it and I was comfortable with it. To incorporate a solar business did not seem very far off from what I was already doing within the electrical aspects of construction. So in a leap of faith, I borrowed $175,000 from one source and $150,000 from a second source not long after.

This probably seems crazy, but I really felt the construction industry crumbling under my feet. I did not believe we had very much time to establish ourselves in the solar business. Up until 2007, I was well known in the building trade only. Relying on word of mouth alone to announce my new involvement in solar would not happen fast enough in my opinion. I bought company vehicles and put well-designed logos on them. We engaged billboards, sponsored sports teams, anything we could to gain exposure. This was all very expensive.

In California, in 2007, the solar industry was just becoming a talked about item. It was hard to find anyone who had installed these products much less a competent contractor to do the service. This industry was literally being born in the private sector. The products were extremely expensive because there was so little demand. As a means to promote the usage of "green" energy the federal government had instituted a sizeable tax credit for those who purchased and installed these items. Likewise, the state of California put together a one-time cash rebate program that was based on a system's size and application (i.e. residential, commercial, etc.)

I can absolutely tell you that it is only due to these incentives that the solar industry ever took hold. For me and my company's involvement I immediately began searching for wholesale outlets to purchase the materials. Assuming this should be relatively easy, I was surprised at the lack of competent wholesale suppliers. You see, everyone was a rookie. This was not, and still is not, an established, secure industry. By 2008, there were a few more wholesalers and contractors joining in, but from my perspective, their reasons were for money not desire.

My first stop in an attempt to establish a relationship with a wholesale supplier found me near Mt. Shasta in Northern California. Traveling interstate 5 in that area regularly, I had seen a billboard for solar products. I called and spoke to the owner. He invited me to stop by so we could talk. Upon my arrival I briefly explained what I was looking for. He spent the next hour bragging. He was not interested in me (a potential long-term client). He wanted an audience to hear how well his company was doing. As I left him that day I wondered if he even knew why I was there. I have not purchased anything from his company nor have I referred them.

Next, I found myself talking to a company closer to my native area in California. They were based in Petaluma, but had opened a small warehouse in Sacramento, which was close to Yolo County where I still reside. I did have a concern with this company that caused some doubt. This was a wholesale company that also sold products to the general public on a retail basis. It has been my experience that it is extremely difficult for a company to do both with a high level of service toward their clients. Never-the-less, they were close to me, I was really needing a supply source and they even offered occasional workshops with representatives from various manufacturers. So I engaged with them. I attended a few of those workshops, called my sales rep regularly with many questions that were usually inadequately answered or not answered at all. Before long I would only get his voicemail. Then he would not return my calls for several days, if at all. Please remember something very important here; **I am trying to buy things from them!** I am the client in this case.

For several months I dealt with this frustration all the while, I am having Marlene search for other wholesale suppliers. Unless I was willing to drive several hours, I was stuck with this company for now. I tried to cope with their complete inadequacies in communication, but finally drew the line when they routinely began to get my orders wrong. That's right; not only would they not return my calls or even answer questions correctly, now they also would regularly package the wrong or incomplete items in my orders.

In total frustration, I insisted to be assigned to a different sales rep. So, I now would talk to Tom. Tom was always responsive and willing to help. He was closer to my age so I believe we had a little more in common which made communicating easier. I soon noticed that if I asked Tom an electronic question about solar modules or inverters, he would need to get back to me later with an answer. Meanwhile the warehouse guys continue to screw up many of my orders, but at least now I have someone I can talk to. Before long it would take Tom until the next day to get back to me with an answer to my previous question. Then pretty soon it was a couple days and so on. Finally I came straight out and asked him why the increasing delay? He said this to me, "I'm really not very knowledgeable with the electrical side of solar. I'm more the solar hot water guy." It turns out he had to ask the same guy I started with any electrical questions about their products. This same guy who would not or could not answer my questions in the first place was now avoiding my questions through Tom. Unbelievable!

Meanwhile back at my office, a young man named Andrew was periodically walking in and soliciting for our business. He would leave his card with Marlene and in turn request a call from me. With experiencing my first year in the solar business the way I had, along with the total disappointment in product support companies, I was disgruntled to say the least. Assuming I would find a similar situation with whoever this "Andrew" was and his company, I did not call him. He kept coming in, always polite and persistent. There was no job title on his business card. The company was "CFM Equipment Distributing". Only the company name and Andrew's name were printed on the card. He continued to stop by and I continued to avoid him. On several occasions Marlene suggested that I should at least talk to him. According to her, he seemed sincere and straightforward. Knowing that the solar business was good for us and that I really wanted to continue pursuing this endeavor, when he happened to stop in one day I decided I had nothing to lose so I sat with him in our front lobby area next to Marlene's desk. Andrew was a very well presented young man in his mid-late 30's. He simply said to me that he would like a chance to earn some of our business. We chatted briefly and he left. I do not remember when we first purchased items from his company, however when we finally did, they got the order right!

I was impressed yet skeptical that this would continue. This was a very large wholesale company that handled heating and air conditioning equipment. They were just beginning to also carry solar products. Due to what I presume was a lack of purchasing power with solar equipment manufacturers, their prices were somewhat higher than the incompetent supplier I had been dealing with. For the next couple of years I kept trying to find a way to buy from Andrew. It was very hard to willingly pay significantly more for the same products, especially since we were also trying to establish ourselves in the solar business. However, Andrew kept coming in and if I called him, he answered immediately or returned my call promptly. If he did not know an answer to my question, he said so and that he would do some research and get back to me soon. This is precisely what he did every time. His integrity seemed to match mine.

Up until now, my impression of others in the solar industry

was one of not knowing and/or not caring. Andrew definitely cared and his learning curve was very rapid. Then the day came when in a typical conversation with one of the other employees and Andrew's company, I learned that he was actually the CEO of that company. When I learned this, I will admit I was surprised. He was very young, he never announced his job title and was a well-spoken and somewhat modest guy. Not the stereotypical CEO by any means. The owner of that company was retiring and did not have a successor. Andrew interviewed and got the job of Chief Executive Officer (CEO) for CFM Equipment Distributing. He, his wife, and daughter moved to California from the east coast because of that job.

As I write this, it was approximately six years ago when I first met Andrew. **If everyone involved in any aspect of the solar industry conducted themselves such as Andrew does, I would not be writing this book. There would be no dishonesty, no incompetence, no greed, no egos, and no conspiracies to talk about. Unfortunately such is not the case.** I am very happy to tell you that Andrew has increased and improved his company. He is now in his early forties and possesses the character that every leader should have. His company is now a main player in the wholesale arena of solar products making their costs extremely competitive. He started a sister company specifically for solar products and it can be found as "U.S. Solar Distributing". To my knowledge, he has outlets on the east coast and the west coast and can supply products to all fifty states. I will say that unless I need a particular product that his company does not handle, I now exclusively buy from Andrew.

I will gladly tie my 30+ year reputation to him with my personal referral. Since our first design and installation of a solar system on a residence in early 2008, my company has installed hundreds of systems on residential, commercial, and agricultural properties. For the first couple of years I bought from multiple wholesale suppliers. Thankfully none have been comparable to that first one. Likewise, none have been comparable to Andrew's company for the opposite reasons.

Before I move on, I must be very clear with my messages here. As I will do throughout these pages and as I have done in all three of my previous books, I only speak true sincere words that come from within. It may sound as though the past few pages were a commercial promoting Andrew and his company. If that is your perspective, I am very good with that. I spoke of Andrew in ways that are based on many years of experience with him personally and his company. He has no previous knowledge of this book. He is completely unaware of these words as I write them. When completed and published, I will personally deliver a signed copy to him. That will be the first awareness he will have of this book.

As you have just learned, my beginning in the solar business was difficult due to the lack of any established history this industry had at that time. Generally speaking, nobody knew what they were doing. Today it is both better and worse. I have shared my beginning as a means to give you a brief understanding of how new this industry is here in America. The overall timing of this industry's birth in the United States has created an irony that is extremely unique. It is precisely the ingredients of the past decade that are responsible for the solar industry becoming a mainstay in growing popularity and, at the same time, the circumstances around the past 6-8 years are precisely what are threatening this industry's future. From a client's perspective, obtaining these products is very easy these days. Unfortunately, the competence and integrity values of many financing and service companies are very questionable. If you are considering a career in solar, your future may be short in this industry if you simply jump on the bandwagon. For those of you who are potential clients and/or career-minded toward the solar industry, I strongly encourage you to open your mind and heart as you continue through this book. I will only deliver true stories and sincere opinions.

CHAPTER 2

Exposure

A s mentioned before, we did just about anything we could to expose our company to the public. Within two years of beginning the solar business, I had five company vehicles full of logos driving around. We purchased several roadside billboard locations, sponsored a local sport team, and participated in many personal appearance events.

Traveling the Shows

One of our distinguishing items was a trailer that I set up as a "rolling classroom". This was an enclosed, tandem axle trailer that was also covered with our logos. On the roof, I mounted four fully functioning solar modules. I used a strong framing method that I custom built to mount the modules on an angle that had them tilted on the trailer roof. This made them obviously visible to anyone whether passing me on the road or walking by when parked.

Along one of the interior walls was a complete mockup of

an installation that included all of the components. Everything was an actual product that represented what would be found in a typical installation. I had several different models of inverters, sub panels, disconnects, conduit, wiring, etc. Found in the front area of the trailers interior were custom-built models of several different mounting methods for both roof and ground frame applications. These were also put together with actual parts and materials. **Authenticity was extremely important to me.** Along the second interior wall Marlene set up hanging basket holders that were stocked with information pamphlets, specification sheets, utility rate structures, cost analysis charts, etc. The trailer had a rear ramp for an entrance and exit that made it very easy for anyone to come in.

For a moving attraction, I used a wooden wine barrel with a 24-inch diameter PVC pipe mounted vertically inside. This I would fill with water and place an actual submersible D.C. well pump inside that operated solely from the solar modules on the trailer's roof. The pump would simply circulate the water up through a pipe that in turn dumped the water back into the barrel. On a hot day at a show, this effect attracted a lot of attention.

Typically, I would set up a pop-up shade cover and a table near the entrance ramp of the trailer. Marlene and I traveled many shows, county fairs and energy workshops with this trailer. For two years we traversed the central and northern valleys of California. Some were a single day and others were multiple days. At locations we felt were important, we would buy space outside for the trailer and also interior building space for a booth. I would occupy the trailer and Marlene would take care of the indoor booth. I cannot remember all the events we attended promoting our company. Some were great fun and others were a complete disappointment. We could have found ourselves assigned a space in the "back forty" of a fairgrounds where it seemed no one knew we were there or we might end up right next to the main gate. You simply never knew. On many occasions I would have people make themselves at home and talk to me for over an hour. Others may stop, grab a card, nod at me, and leave. More than once, the person who spent less time with me at the show would call with additional questions and become a client. The people who had a lot to say, listened very little. They were usually not heard from again.

After two years of this type of exposure, Marlene and I assessed our results. They were not satisfactory. The county fairs were the worst. I concluded that when people attend a fair, they are basically recreating. Being interested in a major purchase such as a solar system was not their mindset at such an event. Also, the few jobs we did get had me and my crew now traveling out of town, so to speak, to complete the work. This meant additional issues. Guys away from home for several days can introduce some interesting challenges in their routines. There were also moderate additional costs with hotels, meals, fuel, etc., not to mention being unfamiliar with locations of hardware stores, equipment rental yards and so on. Although none of these challenges were a surprise to me, they still posed added elements to our endeavors. Remember, during this timeframe I was feeling an urgency to establish my company in the solar industry. I did not believe I could find enough business in my native area of where I resided quick enough, so I was willing to travel. After two years of this type of struggle, I really thought it was best to stay close to home and focus my energy there.

Public Speaking

We had an office on Main Street with a very visible sign, five company vehicles with easy to notice logos, several local billboards and still the incoming business was very modest. In reflecting on all those shows and events in which I had many conversations with a vast diversity of people, it was clear that I really enjoyed the teaching aspect. On many occasions as we were putting away all of our materials at the end of a day at a show, Marlene would comment to me about my discussions with people. She would tell me that it was very obvious when I was "in to it". If I engaged someone who was sincere in their interest, I would expose my passion. I was not "selling", I was "teaching". It has always been my personal priority to help people. For those of you interested in learning the details of what makes me tic, I will refer you to a series of three books I have written called the *Listen* series. These books are my pride and joy professionally speaking. They are delivered with an intuitional connection that is extremely deep. Their titles are: *Listen Without Your Ears, Listen Out Loud, and 20/20 Listening.*

To conclude my own self-promotion here, I wish to say that even though this is my forth book and that it appears much different than my first three books, this book is also tremendously important to me. At the risk of sounding a little corny, there are a lot of "misgivings" in the solar industry that I have had personal exposures to and I truly want to help. My passion of writing is the best way I can potentially help many of you become aware. As I reflected on how I felt when I engaged someone at one of those shows who was genuinely interested, I realized I absolutely loved it! I made a positive difference in that person's knowledge and awareness. Although the reality was that we needed the business, my true passion was found in teaching.

So the question became how to use my passion on a more local basis. Personally I am not comfortable when I am engulfed in a large crowd. However, in certain circumstances, for specific reasons, I can find a place where I feel "into it", as Marlene would put it. Someone we knew belonged to one of the local rotary clubs and it was suggested that I be a guest speaker at one of their luncheons. I accepted and found myself at a podium in front of at least a hundred people for 30 minutes. In my twenties I had done a little speaking in front of a group of community people as a member of a local volunteer fire department but this was much different. Now I was fifty years old and these are all well-known people with all eyes and ears on me.

As I was introduced by the group's chairperson, whom I had known for a long time, it was stated that I was there to talk about solar energy. I could feel the attention span of that audience increase when the chairperson stated what my topic of discussion was. Interest was rapidly growing in solar, yet few knew much about it. I began with a brief introduction and just a few minutes of basic definitions. Then I said I would really like to spend our time with questions they may have. Well, many hands went up and the questions were not in limited supply. When the chairperson had to interrupt to say that our time was up, she did so apologetically. There were still hands in the air and, if I may say so myself, the feeling was that these people wanted to continue. That 30 minutes seemed like 5 minutes to me. These people were really interested in my responses and on many occasions I could see clarity on their faces as we conversed. They were getting it! It was obvious they had not been exposed to such straightforward talk without a display of salesmanship. As I ate lunch with them, a few talked to me privately and thanked me for my approach and what they considered valuable information.

After this experience I realized that I have something I can use for a mutual benefit to all. I love to teach. If I can help people understand the actual value in solar products without all the *B.S.* that is rapidly increasing in this industry, they will be better prepared to make good intelligent decisions and my company may gain a few clients. So I did this on a somewhat regular basis. I spoke to multiple rotary clubs in the a.m., afternoon and p.m. meeting times, lions clubs, energy fairs as one of the guest speakers etc. Some of these groups were little more than a dozen people with others well over 100 people. As long as I was at a podium talking about the products and business of solar, I was in my groove.

I do not remember if we realized very many new clients due to my many podium visits. However, I cannot tell you how much satisfaction I gained because I was sincerely helping others understand the reality of solar. I will also disclose to you that I actually learned a lot also. I learned about me. I learned that I have capabilities that had been suppressed up until I was placed at those podiums. I will always prefer to write, but in certain situations, for specific reasons, I can engage a large group of people.

Large Scale Attempt

By 2010, things were changing rapidly for me. I had restructured my company by now to give it a face of solar design and installation. Although we occasionally still dabbled in the construction arena, my focus was all on solar. Some of my old construction employees went away, others adapted to solar, and a few new employees were hired specifically for our solar endeavors. We would have months of plentiful work and cash flow and then there were those times of nothing. This rollercoaster ride of business volume made it very difficult to plan. Just when I would wonder if that was it, we were done, the phone would ring and a client materialized. Trying to maintain some form of planned control when the incoming business is so radical is very stressful. I remember days that Marlene would show up bubbly and smiling and then other days she looked as though she just came from a funeral.

With what I felt was a very good installation crew in place and in an attempt to finally break out and realize sustained business, we made a big decision. We would create a radio commercial. This was a big deal to us. We had been through several years of unpredictable volume, already done the "traveling" thing and here we were talking about a large scale exposure that could take us 150 miles in any direction. Nervous about committing thousands of dollars, that we never really knew if we would have at any given time, the risk taker in me plunged ahead. The first choice was which station to use. Our office in Woodland was very near Sacramento which housed many radio stations. Most of these stations were within a listener base population of over a million people. We carefully and strategically analyzed who our clients were. Primarily between forty and seventy years old, good career, homeowner, typically well informed etc. I did not want to choose a type of music genre that was real specific such as rock or county due to a concern of limited access to our "bracket" of clients. Likewise, I was not interested in news or talk radio because of its negative nature. Solar is supposed to represent a positive, so I wanted an audience that was in a good mood.

Let me be clear on my comment toward rock and/or county radio stations. The reality was that rock tends to attract younger people that do not buy solar (yet). Also, to be completely honest, many country listeners (of which I have been for most of my life) tend to be very conservative. At that point in time most forms of "green" energy were very non-traditional, therefore bared a stereotype of being "liberal" in political terms. I will say that this stereotype is rapidly fading away. Having a choice, where only a utility monopoly existed before is very American wouldn't you say?

So in reality we chose a radio station by the process of elimination. We settled on a station that played the classics. Focusing on the music from the 60's, 70's, 80's and primarily on the "easy rock" portions of those decades. The listener base of this well-known Sacramento station fit the description of our clientele. They had a very diversified group of personalities. Some of their D.J.'s had been in the business 40 years and others were not even born when this music was popular. We found their staff very pleasant and easy to work with. There was one D.J. in particular that was their early morning guy (6am – 9am). I remember hearing him on a country station in Sacramento when I was in high school in the mid-seventies. I grew up in a very rural setting in Yolo County and the Sacramento stations were the only ones we could get. He is a very talented and funny guy named Joey Mitchell. I ended up shooting a video with him that can be viewed on one of my websites: www. solarintegrity.net.

In the actual creation of the 30-second ad, I worked with two other on-air personalities. Both were very talented and patient with me. The end product had me introducing myself and my company and making a few statements. Then one of the D.J.'s joined in with a few statements and then I finished up. My style in that commercial was authentically who I am. With a very similar approach as I presented during all those podium talks that produced extremely positive feedback, I expected good response.

This ad was clear, concise, honest and to the point. I did not offer prizes or giveaways. I simply spoke with integrity. This ad ran on air 15-20 times each day during a mixture of am, mid-day and evening times. It was played for 2½ months during the late summer and early fall, which was the busy season for solar interest. My ad was the first and only solar ad this station had. A few of the "mega" solar companies were beginning to use radio, but had not yet done so with this station. Since my introductory radio ad for solar with this station took place in 2010, many solar companies now use this station. In fact, too many in my opinion. I do not believe it is good for a station to allow so much redundancy with very similar ads that seemingly run back to back. However, I am not in the radio business.

To recap briefly, we created and ran a 30-second ad on a very popular radio station in Sacramento, California for 2½ months during peak listening days and times and in the busy season for solar. This station had an audience that primarily coincided with our clientele base and incorporated their on-air personalities with my personal statements. This came at a cost of well over $6,000.

Before I continue, I want to pose a very sincere question to all of you. Is there anything else you would have considered or done if you were in charge of making a radio commercial? I believe most of you think that I covered all the bases. I do realize that you have not heard the content or delivery of that ad, so all I can tell you is that it appeared to be very good. I was extremely happy with it. My employees and the radio stations staff all approved. With every bit of sincere honesty, I will tell you **it attracted zero. Not one call. Not one email. Not one person walked in our office on Main Street because of this ad. Not even a single prank call.** If I had not heard it many times myself on the radio, I may have accused the station of not playing it. I was absolutely amazed! How is this even possible? This simply doesn't happen, but it did.

After this sank in, I felt like I was nearly out of options. I had invested over three years of exhausting attempts to establish a sustained business in an industry that provided overwhelming compliments toward me from my existing clients and from my teaching exposures, yet it was as though it was not meant to be. Well, actually I was not consciously aware of what was coming then, but now it is as clear as spring water to me.

CHAPTER 3

Big Changes

The radio commercial was my biggest and last significant attempt to grow my solar business. By 2010 there was a single ingredient that was taking this industry by storm and I quickly knew I did not want to be associated with it at all. The solar lease.

The Perfect *Solar* Storm

When you really consider all the circumstances that came together between 2006 and 2009, which basically created our current direction in this industry collectively, it is incredible to realize the dramatic effects they had then and still have now. At the front of this line is the housing market. During the earliest years of this century a situation was created that will become history for many future generations to read about. Money became cheap and available. By 2004, nearly anyone could qualify for a home loan. Also, many loans were structured and approved that far exceeded the borrowers reasonable capability to repay. Like a balloon that was inflated way too quickly, the housing market popped. It was officially reported as collapsed in 2008, but I felt it start to go in mid-2006. By 2007 it seemed obvious to me, at least in Northern California, that things were headed down.

The total number of careers that became dependent on the crazy boom of this country's housing market during those few years is staggering. All of the real estate and land sectors, the complete construction industry that included builders, plumbers, electricians, roofers, lumber and material providers and suppliers along with everything else connected to building a structure, etc. However, as huge of an impact as was created when all of these sectors collapsed, none was more important to our collective future as was the collapse of money.

The amount of money that was flowing through the housing market in 2004 and 2005, and even through 2006, was utterly ridiculous. When this came to an abrupt end, all those investors along with their opportunistic priorities were homeless. The smart investors that got out prior to losing their collateral and/ or cash now had nowhere to go. The only thing a big money person likes less than stagnant money is losing money. When the financing stopped, money became stagnant. This meant no financial growth. If you simply stuff your cash under your mattress, it loses value each day due to inflation, which in turn dictates buying power. Three thousand dollars in the 1970's would buy a new car. Now it takes thirty thousand dollars. So our **first ingredient** in our brewing storm that was destined to impact the solar industry is the **collapse of the U.S. housing market, which left many investors stranded.**

Our next impact was created within the work force. Seemingly overnight there were a huge number of people unemployed. Real estate agents, construction workers, bank loan officers, landscapers, road workers, etc. The rapid influx of people looking for the next thing to build or install or maintain was dramatic to say the least. So this becomes our **second ingredient** in our oncoming storm. **Out of work blue collar workers and sales people** desperately in need of a job.

The third players in this unique phenomenon were all the support industries. Basically this means warehouses, wholesale suppliers, manufactures, etc. These people make the products, warehouse them and supply the builders/installers who sell and install these products to the end user (client) who has taken out a loan to pay for it from the investor. So these huge warehouses on the outskirts of most big towns and cities were becoming empty. Previously stocked with materials to support the housing boom, the demand vanished leaving them without a product to stock and sell. Now we have identified our **third ingredient** in our major fictitious weather event. **Empty warehouses** looking for something to carry.

Now we have reached our supporting cast of players. These are the people and departments that usually go unnoticed by the general public. Typically in the public sector, these are building departments, planning departments, health and public works departments, etc. Budgets were cut, people laid off, attitudes diminished and familiar exposures drastically reduced. So our **fourth ingredient** in the developing storm that will manifest itself into the solar industry is **diminished public servants. Not only diminished in numbers but more importantly a reduced attitude and competence level in those who remained.** Add to this a very limited quantity of these folks had ever been exposed to solar products or their application. Because solar usage in this country was virtually non-existent in the private sector prior to 2006, there were very few regulations to speak of for these people to refer to. Their "bible" is typically their department's code book. Without a code to read, many of these people are lost. (And these are the good ones.)

Now we have come to our **fifth and final circumstance** that brought together the impending storm that left in its wake the solar industry of current times. **Created desire without reasonable means.** Let me explain. Who installs the most solar? Homeowners. What happened to a huge number of homeowners after the housing market crashed? Many of them lost the homes they couldn't afford in the first place. However, there is another very large group of people that played a **major role in the coming solar industry. These were the homeowners that actually kept their houses, but lost all their equity.** In fact, a large portion of this second group were quickly upside-down in their homes' value. Along with this drastic devaluing of their home, many of them realized damaged credit scores due to a debt structure that they created based on borrowed money against their home. It was very easy to have a line of credit on the house and buy a boat for example. So when the value of the house dropped in half nearly overnight, the line of credit was worthless because the loan that was in "1st place", which was the primary mortgage, was higher than the total value of the house. The boat ended up being repossessed, which left the credit score of the homeowner severely damaged. This homeowner kept making the house payment and retained their home, but all the other debt associated likely suffered. So our **fifth ingredient is homeowners with no equity** and possibly damaged credit scores. As time passed, the credit scores were repaired much quicker than the equities. In fact, home equity was stagnant for several years. Credit scores, on the other hand, can be rebuilt in 2-3 years relatively easy with a little management. We now have everything needed to realize a perfect solar storm and that is precisely what materialized.

It All Came Together

Let's list our five ingredients in order to understand what came next as we examine this occurrence.

1. The collapse of the housing market left a lot of money with nowhere to go.
2. Massive quantities of unemployed blue collar workers and sales people.
3. Warehouses and suppliers, along with certain manufactures, without products to make and distribute.
4. Public support departments trained for the construction industry lacking knowledge in the solar industry. Also an on slot of diminished attitudes driven by the uncertainty of a professional future.
5. A massive clientele base of homeowners without equity and possibly damaged credit. The general public was without buying power on a large scale.

To put this in perspective with an easy to visualize analogy, consider a rollercoaster. When taking a ride on a typical rollercoaster, the first experience is the somewhat slow, steady climb much the same as the housing market between 2003 and 2006. Prices kept going up and up. The illusion was that this trend would continue. Somewhere along the way, the prices exceeded a reasonable market value and from that point on it was only a created value on paper. As 2006 progressed and moved into 2007 the housing market had reached its highest point and began to slowly tip over the top and head in a very gradual descending direction. Much like a rollercoaster as it tops out. You know what is coming, but aren't quite there yet. Then, in what seems like the blink of an eye, you see the tracks disappear in front of you and down you go. As the housing market turned the calendar to 2008, this is just what happened. There was no time to reconsider or grab a hold of any safety bar, it was simply straight down! This freefall took five years to travel. Only in the last year or so has the housing market shown real signs of stability and even a slow ascend.

So what does all this have to do with our current solar direction? At the beginning of this chapter I stated that a single ingredient was taking the solar industry by storm. This single thing has completely shaped the way the majority of homeowners obtain solar currently. It is precisely this one presence that I believe will soon become a major threat to the continued growth and popularity of solar usage in the private sector. **The solar lease was created and has become the "face" of the entire industry precisely because of all the ingredients we have identified throughout this chapter.**

> *Remove any one of the five ingredients except possibly number four, the public support issues, and the solar industry does not become what it is today in 2014. If the housing market doesn't crash, the money stays there and there are very few investors to push a lease into existence. If all the contractors keep building houses, few would have incorporated solar due to a lack of customer demand. Likewise, the warehouses are still full of components to support all the construction trades. Finally we realize that the equities are primarily still intact so those few who would have desired solar would simply borrow and purchase it themselves. A 15-20 year rental contract would not be attractive at all.*

Collectively we have been moving toward a "greener" position for quite some time. Remove our "perfect solar storm" and the solar market does happen, but at a much slower rate. This current "bubble" of rapid solar increase was manufactured primarily by the big money investors who recognized a tremendous opportunity to capitalize. They had all the necessary ingredients to create the frenzy that has materialized. There was an available and hungry work force. The client could not borrow and purchase the expensive equipment up front. Manufacturing and distribution needed something to do. Like ducks on a pond, this was easy picking for "money and power" to create a situation whereas a lease was the only way for many to obtain a "green" product that was very aggressively marketed to them. To top it all off, the government made their endeavor nearly risk free.

Incentives

The federal government had created an extremely attractive tax credit in an attempt to promote "green" energy usage. I wish to be clear in this understanding so I will explain. There was and still is, as of the time of this writing, a thirty percent federal tax credit toward any U.S. citizen who **owns** an approved alternative energy system. The key word in this statement is "owns". For example: If you purchase and install a functioning solar system on your property, and it cost $30,000 to complete, you are eligible to receive a $9,000 Federal Tax Credit, providing you have paid or will owe at least that amount in income taxes. The tax credit **follows the equipment** not the location. In other words, whoever owns the equipment, regardless of where it is installed, receives the tax credit. Therefore, by retaining ownership of the equipment, the leasing company can indeed install **their equipment** on your property and they receive the tax credit, not you. Sounds really good for the leasing company doesn't it? But wait, there is more. If the equipment becomes part of a business, the business owner can also depreciate the remaining balance of the costs after the 30% tax credit is deducted. Much the same as when a farmer buys a tractor, the farmer can depreciate the cost of the tractor as a part of conducting his business. A leasing company's business is obviously the equipment they are "renting out" so-to-speak, therefore the solar equipment that **they** own and that is part of their conducting a business is eligible for both the 30% Federal Tax Credit and a depreciation value based on their tax structure. At this point many of you will assume that I do not approve of this type of financial arrangement. On the contrary, I do not have any problem with such a relationship **if** it is approached with integrity. Herein we find the issues.

"We Promise"

If you go down to your local car dealership and buy a new Ford, it will come with a warranty. If you finance your new car through a bank, who is providing you with the car's warranty? Well, I can tell you it is definitely not the money people. The warranty comes from the smart people who have built and understand the product. In this case, Ford. With this type of guarantee you are probably very comfortable. Ford is well established. Everyone has heard of this company. They have a reputation that is very old and deep. Consider this: If the banker was the one guaranteeing the proper function of the car for so many years, how confident are you now? What does a banker know about the function and longevity of that car? Let's keep going in this direction for a little longer. Now, what if Ford said that they will warranty **their** car for 5 years, but the state stepped in and demanded that Ford increase the warranty time to 10 years if they want to keep selling cars in that state? Wait, there is still one more step. So now the banker is going to lease you the car for 20 years and by doing so is promising you that the car will function for this entire term of the lease. Let's recap this scenario briefly.

1. The people who built the car said 5 years.
2. The state bureaucracy said no, it must be 10 years.
3. The financing entity said, wait a minute, we created a contract for 20 years so the warranty must match; it's 20 years.

Remember something very important here; **the mechanics of the car did not change.** Of these three entities, who do you believe knows the most about the car? Better yet; **why would you sign a 20 year contract that guarantees a product for a period of time which the actual manufacturer said is much less?** Many people have signed such a contract, and many more will continue to do so. **This is the promise of a solar lease.** In the next chapter, we will examine in detail what I believe is on the horizon for many of these types of relationships between a leasing company and the client.

In closing this chapter I would like to take you through my exposures with solar leases and my abrupt parting of the ways with one company in particular.

My Brief Encounter

By 2010 it was obvious that if my company was to gain any form of consistent volume with a good flow of clients we would need an attractive finance tool. After the housing crash, banks basically went underground. The average homeowner stood very little chance of actually being approved for a loan. The traditional banking industry did not understand the value in solar equipment and would not even consider creating a financing product for it. I can tell you this from personal experience. I'll bet Marlene and I met with officers from 7 or 8 different banks and/or credit unions in search of a program we could offer our clients. Although some reacted favorably during our meeting, not one ever materialized. We did come across a small credit union in Napa Valley, California that indeed had a solar loan program. This was a legitimate loan which had the client purchasing the equipment. As soon as we got going with their program, they discontinued it. I think we only ended up with two completed projects through them. The bottom line was that lending institutions were very skeptical about loaning anyone any amount unless that client really didn't need the loan in the first place.

With nowhere else to look, I decided to investigate some of the leasing products in case there may be an actual good one. We looked at several and it became very redundant. They were extremely similar. Most of them had us doing the install and then getting paid within 30 days. This I would not and could not do. In a 30-day timeframe it was very feasible for us to potentially install $100,000 worth of systems. This would mean that we would have fronted that much before getting paid for the first job 30 days prior. Like I said, I would not and could not do that.

Then we contacted a company that was based in California and was actually a manufacturer of solar modules. They had recently came out with their own in-house lease that was exclusively used for their listed contractors using only their equipment. This one intrigued me. They were not just bankers, they were first and foremost equipment people. Although their modules were too overpriced to simply buy them outright, I wanted to actually look at the nuts and bolts of their lease product. The first hurdle we faced was that I was not one of their listed or approved contractors. They typically operated based on territories so to not have their chosen few competing with each other. Although there was one of their approved installers less than 15 miles from our office, apparently his volume wasn't adequate because they did accept us.

So I approached this potential new relationship with extreme caution. I had a 30+ year personal reputation in this area that I was and still am very protective of. **Under no circumstances would I allow anyone else to dictate my priorities.** Right from the start we had issues, however they seemed willing to be flexible so we continued. There were two beginning issues that I recall. One was "lead time" to fill an order. They told me to allow 3 weeks for them to process my order for equipment. I was accustomed to 3 days from other distributors. I agreed to a week with a 10 day maximum. I do not make my clients wait any longer than my schedule dictates. I would not compromise this because of their less than adequate approach.

I mentioned earlier that their lease program was relatively new. Well it must have been because Marlene found several errors and/or contradictions in their contracts. Whoever drew up those contracts was not efficient, and this was no small company. However, yet again they were flexible and adjusted the language on those few items in the contracts. Although there were similarities, there were two contracts. One was between us and them and the other was for the client which included us and them. Still a little skeptical, I convinced myself that this was as good as it will get with any financing tool that was available. At least this company had their own hardware involved, which I figured made them more concerned about the future. The inverters they put their name on were built buy a well-known manufacturer. This company only made modules. So away we went!

We quickly had one job to do within this new relationship and before long we also had a second and third waiting. With the first job completed and the client for the next job ready to go, including their signed contract, something happened. The company rep contacted us and requested we change the module type and model on job number two. I asked Marlene to inquire as to why. **We already had a contract with the client spelling out the equipment.** When we were unable to get a straight answer, I became resistant. I would not go back to **my** client and suggest an equipment change for no apparent reason. All they had to do was give me a legitimate reason I could forward to my client. They remained very vague (with me). It seems they contacted my sales manager and asked him to persuade me. He had attempted such things before without success. It wasn't his reputation we were dealing with, it was mine! Finally the rep told my sales manager that they were recalling that particular module and wanted to keep it quiet to avoid any client concerns. So instead, they wanted me to lie to my client. **Not going to happen!** When I learned of this, I called Marlene and requested she immediately send an email to that rep stating that we are to be removed from their contractor list at once. I would not associate my company or myself with this absence of integrity.

So now that we had actually participated in a lease contract, we knew what to look for and what questions to ask any other leasing companies we may look into. This produced very interesting results. Some would not even let us see a contract before we made a commitment to them. As I really began to put together the common denominators, I realized some very disturbing similarities. In the next chapter I will detail what these are along with my opinions on where this is all heading.

CHAPTER 4

Secrets of the Lease

Let's begin this chapter with something that is not a secret at all. Here is a very common question that I am asked frequently. What if I decide to sell my house after I put solar on it? I answer this question by segregating it into two parts. First, if the solar system was initially purchased outright, the real estate transaction should be smooth. This will have everything to do with the quality of the installation along with various other factors such as the systems age, size, etc. If the solar system is relatively young (less than 10 years old) it should add a value to the selling amount. For people who install a moderately sized system, that reduces or eliminates a significant utility cost, I suggest that they keep a few of their previous utility bills as a reference for any potential buyers.

Here in my part of California we are within the very large utility jurisdiction known as Pacific Gas & Electric Company (PG&E). This utility is one of three public utilities in the state and is the largest of all the utilities in California. In fact, PG&E is one of the largest utilities in the country. Coexisting with privately owned solar systems that are attached to the grid is very common for this utility. I will tell you that my company has directly tracked the many different rate structures within this utility since the year 2000 to establish a basis that we use in our cost analysis and return on investment (ROI) projections that we provide to our clients. Marlene began with the new year of this millennia as a starting point to develop averages for all the PG&E rates that our potential clients would pay. For 14 years we have kept up these averages for all of the rate structures that apply to our clients. In round numbers, the average annual cost inflation rate of the residential utility costs within the PG&E structure run between 6% and 7% of an increase each year. If you put this into a flow chart as we do, you would find that the average utility cost for the average residence within PG&E territory doubles every 11 years or so. This means that if an average residence is paying $2,000/year in utility electric costs, it will gradually increase to $4,000/year eleven years from now. This will become very important information a little later in our discussion, but for now, you can see the value in keeping a few of the previous utility bills to show potential home buyers.

The second part of my answer to the "what if I sell" question addresses a solar system that was not initially purchased, but rather leased and has an ongoing contract attached to the equipment. There is a fundamental realization that is very important when installing a solar system anywhere on your property. **It is permanent**. The solar equipment is not portable. This means it is attached on the basis that it remains. When someone moves to or from a house, certain things can go while others do not. The refrigerator is portable, the built-in oven is not. The laundry units are likely portable, the central heat and air units are not. You get the picture. If the property is altered by removing something that has been bolted on, wired in, plumbed in, etc. then those items are considered permanent.

Obviously a solar system is both "bolted on" and "wired in". In my opinion, when buying or selling a property that has a "permanent" item attached to it, with a remaining open contractual obligation also attached to it and it is not "owned" by the seller, a much more confusing and difficult transaction awaits.

The "Eye" of the Storm

Now we are going to focus our attention on one specific component in every solar system: The inverter(s). The majority of all discussions around solar comes by way of the modules. This what everybody talks about. It is easy to understand why too. The modules absolutely dominate the visual aspect of any system. They take up the vast majority of the space required. They constitute the single largest cost within a system. There are literally hundreds of makes and models to choose from (so far). Also, quite frankly this is what has become the focal point of all the different marketing angles. Well, guess what? When considering a lease, it is not the modules that are going to produce what I believe are very significant issues in our near future. **The coming problems are going to center around a leased systems inverter(s).**

The irony is, that in the initial stages of deciding whether to purchase or lease, most people spend little or no time investigating the inverter(s). That is because this component kind of goes unnoticed. A solar array that might fill your roof with modules may only have one inverter hanging on a wall somewhere that is smaller than the average suitcase. The inverter provides very little, if any, visual impact and quite honestly most people (including most sales people) do not understand its function. However, if you are considering a lease, I encourage you to focus primarily on the inverter(s).

> *Here's why. Since the car analogy worked so well before, let's use it again. If we cross-referenced a car and a functioning solar system, it would go like this. The modules, which everyone wants to talk about, are the engine. They are the power source. If you went out to buy a car, once you got past the initial visual impact along with the equipment you wanted the car to include, you would likely turn your attention to the engine. After all it is the engine that provides the necessary power for the car to operate. Let me pose a question. How much attention, if any, would you give to the transmission? Most of you would skip right past that component. Why? Simple. The sales people do not talk about it, it is not visual (you have to crawl under the car just to see it) and it seldom comes up in any decision to obtain a vehicle. Now consider this: You can have the most beautiful car, full of all the options known to man, with a million horsepower engine, but without the transmission, the wheels will never turn. The solar modules are the "engine" of a functioning system. They provide the generated power. The inverter is the "transmission". Without this, the system will never "go".*

D.C. into A.C.

If you follow me with this next part, it will be easy to understand why the inverter is actually the center of attention. I will try to avoid becoming too technical. In the very early part of the twentieth century there was a debate within the powers-to-be about which type of electrical power is best, A.C. (alternating current) or D.C. (direct current). To keep this discussion very simple, you can differentiate these two in this way. Alternating Current (A.C.) can move the constant flow of power much greater distances and with much smaller wires than can Direct Current (D.C.) power. So with this information alone, you can quickly understand why it was the A.C. form of power that was adopted for widespread power delivery in this country in those early days. Likewise, it is A.C. power that has become a standard in most countries around the world.

So why is this important in our discussion here? The solar modules (the power generating engine) produce **D.C.** power as they gather the sunlight. The inverter (the transmission) is the absolutely necessary device that transforms (inverts) the D.C. power from the modules into **A.C.** power that is compatible with our grid and all the typical components that use power. Without an inverter the solar modules have no outlet for their power when attached to the standard form of A.C. power supplies, such as the grid, or any of the typical things that use power. So even though the inverter is not very visible or only poses a small portion of the overall initial costs, it is the "heart beat" of a functioning system.

Remember earlier when we talked about warranties by using the new Ford car analogy? I also stated that my analogy was the premise of the solar lease. Let's once again visit the warranty issue, only we will use a solar inverter in place of the car. In this case I am referring to what are known as "string" inverters, which are the most commonly used. This type of method has a single inverter that is attached to a group of modules. There are other methods that we will discuss later, but I will stay with the most popular method for now. In our new focus of inverter warranties, in conjunction with a typical lease agreement, notice the similarity to our car analogy from earlier.

When it comes to solar usage in general, the U.S. is the new kid on the block. Many of the European countries have been installing privately owned systems for decades. In Germany for example, owning your own solar system is very commonplace. Thus, it is easy to understand why most of the tried and proven inverter technologies originated there. Today, the two largest inverter manufacturers both have German decent. When it comes to building inverters, they know what they are doing. When I first began my solar company in 2007, an inverter came in a box that had a warranty printed on the outside. It said 5-year warranty. When the state of California instituted the one-time cash rebate program between 2005–2006, it was decided that because rebates were being paid out, the warranty should be longer. So it was the politicians that decided these same inverters should have a 10 year warranty. Forced into this or do not sell their product in California, the inverter folks agreed to the 10 year warranty.

Finally, when the "perfect solar storm" hit and the lease was born, it could only be presented in an attractive way to the client by extending the payment structure out to 20 years. If a shorter payment structure was used, the monthly lease payment would exceed the amount of the utility cost that was being offset by the leased system. This would have meant higher monthly costs with a solar system that was leased versus a continuation of simply paying the utility bill. Not an easy sell by any means. It is only because of the monthly payment structure that the lease term has been at 20 years typically. I have recently heard of one company that has realigned their structure to a 15-year term.

This is too little, too late. In a future chapter I will disclose a business plan that Marlene and I spent considerable time developing at the request of a group of community leaders who were pursuing a broad scale collective endeavor. This plan was extremely positive! In fact, I referred to it as a "triple-win".

The client won in a big way. This was a **12-year** lease plan that always had the client's monthly lease payment amount considerably less than the previous utility bill that was being offset. Also, the manufacturer warranty and lease terms were much more aligned. The community group/investment group made a very good profit which would put them in a position to help low-income clients obtain solar also. My company realized the potential for a moderate increase in sustained volume. It was a win-win-win situation and all done so within **12 years**, while the widely used leases were all at 20 years.

However, for now let's stay focused on the warranty aspect of the traditional solar lease. In order to feed the overhead of their big machines, **the numbers forced these big leasing companies to stretch out the terms to 20 years, but there was a problem. The inverter only had a 10-year warranty.** How could they convince people to sign such a long-term agreement if they could not also convince them that the system will continue to produce power and offset their utility bill? After all, the reality is that the vast majority of those who obtain solar, do so with a priority of financial gain. The "green" aspect is not the deciding factor for most people. So the only real challenge to having this new tremendous opportunity to profit was found in **equipment longevity.** It is at this point that I am going to go into "conspiracy mode", which is very uncommon for me in general. But knowing what I know, along with what I have been exposed to in this industry, I truly believe I "smell a rat".

The 20/10 Plan

I will give you the punch line first, and then go into the details of explaining the joke as I believe it to be. The financial wizards examined every angle they could think of when approaching the lease potential. It always pointed toward 20 years. To get the "money people" the return they demanded, along with the short-term exposure of risk they required, it was inevitable that it would take 20 years to structure a product that would accomplish this, while also being attractive to the average client with persuasive salesmanship. So they say "out loud" in their contracts, "We guarantee production" from **our** equipment to offset some or all of **your** utility costs for the term of the lease (20 years).

> *Look familiar to our earlier analogy? Manufacturer = 5 years, state bureaucracy = 10 years, financing entity = 20 years. Ask yourself these questions: Of these three entities, who stands to gain the most financially? Contrary to your likely answer, who do you trust the most? Two different answers aren't they? So what is the punch line? They say 20 years, but are really planning on 10. Why only 10 years you ask? Remember the length of the inverter warranty prior to the lease? That's right, it is 10 years. I'll bet it is all beginning to clear up for most of you now.*

The Five Scenarios

Now I would like to go through what I believe are the four likely scenarios, along with an additional situation that will apply to a portion of the lease/client relationships. Let's start with the best case potential and then work our way down.

1. Your leased system is a little less than 10 years old when the inverter stops working. You immediately grab the phone and call the leasing company. They are actually still in business and a real person answers your call. (I already do not believe this). Their response with a service person to your property is very quick. They confirm a bad inverter and a new one is on its way. A few days later the service person returns with your replacement inverter and your system is back online.

Now allow me to explain why I think this scenario is a fairy tale. Currently most of these leasing companies are very busy installing. What this means is that there are a lot of systems scattered over a large geographical area that sooner or later will have issues. This means that the second group of 10 years in this company's existence will realize a very large volume of service calls. It is extremely unlikely that an inverter will go for the full 20 years of a lease contract. At some point during the 8-12 year mark, it is a very good bet that the inverter will go out. Because the client is "guaranteed power production" for the term of the lease, all of the service call costs are the burden of the leasing company and/or the installation contractor.

As a long time contractor myself, I cannot imagine that there are any contractors out there who are installing these systems under a lease agreement that makes them personally responsible for the warranty work for 20 years. If there

are, I do not have confidence in their future. In my experience, inverter companies that replace inverters within the 10-year warranty period will pay a contractor a flat service fee of $150-$250. I have yet to see one higher than $250. How motivated do you think these leasing companies will be to run around with company vehicles and paid service techs for $250? **Not at all** is the correct answer. So even if the inverter is still under the 10-year manufacturer's warranty, getting the proper person to replace it is going to be a real challenge. But wait, this is only the beginning of the potential issues.

Remember our discussion around the average utility inflation in their rates to the client? With PG&E in California, the average annual residential inflation rate is between 6-7%. So now let's consider your utility bill once again.

The day your leased system was put online, your utility cost for electricity either dropped or went away all together. Over the past 8 or 9 years, you have become very accustomed to this. You are not even aware of what your bill would be after this many years because the solar has worked so well. You remember the first month you had your newly **rented** system and how your utility bill went down by $150 (hypothetically) that first month. So now 9 years later you realize that your (actually it is theirs) inverter is offline. When you called to report this, you got a machine. A few days later still no return call. You call again and leave a little more abrupt message. Now a week has gone by and you finally get a return call. They will send someone out in a "few days". Another week goes by and you are very frustrated. You call again. You get a return call promptly that is apologizing for the delay. You calm down because you feel a form of control now that they have paid attention to you. You are promised a visit next week. Now at the end of your third "unproductive" week a technician shows up. "Yep, your inverter is bad" you are told. A new one is ordered and they will call you when it arrives to schedule a replacement date. A week later, the call comes in and a date is scheduled for the middle part of next week. The technician shows up and replaces the bad inverter some 5 weeks after you first reported it. Guess what? You just got a utility bill in the mail for the past month. Remember, 9 years ago it would have been $150. Now it is $275!

I truly believe that this scenario described above will be the **best-case** scenario.

2. This scenario has the leasing company still in business; only your report to them about your down inverter comes beyond the 10-year manufacturer warranty period. Now what? Remember your contract "guarantees power production" for the term of the lease. I will repeat an earlier question. How motivated will they be **now** to repair the inverter issue? Not only do they have to purchase a replacement, they do not even get the $250 service rate. Also, what does that surprise utility bill that you are getting due to the lengthy downtime look like now? Remember, on average, in our example, it doubled every 11 years or so. Ouch!

3. This scenario has you waiting for the return call and/or a replacement inverter for a very long time. Meanwhile your newly acquired utility costs are piling up. You finally reach a frustration level that has you taking

matters into your own hands. You are going to find a service tech yourself and pay for a new inverter and the labor to install it. But wait, you can't! **You do not own it.** Therefore, you cannot authorize the work without written permission from the owners of the equipment. With this realization, you have reached genuine anger. You decide that you are not making any more monthly lease payments. Unfortunately, there is a contract obligating you to continue the payments. I know, I completely agree. Those x?!$# are not keeping up their end of the deal! If you discontinue making the payments, what eventually happens? Collections? Credit score damage? Attorneys? Lawsuits?

4. You call to report that your inverter is not working. The number has been disconnected. I cannot even begin to suggest how this one will end up. However, realistically I believe this will not end well. The lease company has vanished. The contractors who installed systems under their agreement have a lot of very upset clients. If the lease company had their own labor force doing the installations, those people are out of a job and also not very appreciated by the clients. I believe that no more needs to be said in this case.

5. An additional situation that I believe is likely to happen is going to be the creation of "repair contractors". As of this year (2014), we have yet to see any trucks running around with a logo that says, "Solar repair". This will soon change. If I were just now contemplating a career in the construction part of the solar industry, I would definitely consider the repair side. This will become in high demand in a few years as all the scenarios we

just went through begin to unfold. There will be one major issue to figure out though and we have already touched on it. **The legality of who owns the equipment and who can authorize work on it.** If an initial company installs it, but another company works on it, the assumption of remaining warranties becomes a real concern. So although I believe solar repair companies are on the horizon, it will take some well thought out arrangements to protect everyone involved when the equipment is not actually owned by the property owner.

Beyond these scenarios that refer to the traditional solar lease in which the client is renting the equipment for an established length of time only, there is yet a different type of lease known as a "Power Purchase Agreement" (PPA). These become much more complicated. I recently received a copy of such an agreement from someone I know. Of the 16 pages in this contract, only 2 or 3 had the "blanks" filled in to reflect the individual circumstances. The other 13 or 14 pages were all pre-printed legal do's and don'ts. A lot of guarantees and promises are made. There was zero mention of any of the equipment specifications, quantities, etc. The only thing the client saw was a flow chart with the annual progressive estimated kWh (kilowatt hour) production. If the solar system did not make its minimum allotted production quantity for any particular year, the lease company would refund the difference. What's not to like about that?

Partway through all of the "clauses" and "sections", I found something that struck me as very troublesome. This lease company has **full authority and discretion to transfer, sell, or give away any portion or all of the contractual obligations.** In other words, the lease company does not have to see the 20 year contract all the way through; they can remove themselves without the clients' consent toward any other company. The PPA is marketed and "sold" as a means to "guarantee" the client they will remain in business. They accomplish this by saying that it is their produced power from the solar that the client is buying from the lease company, therefore this company is motivated to keep the system operational so they have produced power to sell to the client.

This may indeed prove to be true in some cases down the road, but now let me share some of the round numbers attached to this particular case. By seeing the first year's estimated kWh production, I was able to calculate a very close estimate of the actual size of this system. I am also familiar with the location of the client so I am very confident of my size calculations. Later in this book we will discuss average costs, sizes, etc., but for now I will simply say that an expected cost for the total of all the equipment and labor for this estimated system would be approximately $38,000. If this client was actually purchasing the system, they would be eligible to receive an $11,400 tax credit, thus reducing their invested amount to $26,600. By examining the various "pre-pay" or "purchase" options that were offered in the contract, I could work backwards and uncover (in close proximity) the depreciation amounts that the lease company intends to claim. By the time I added the estimated installation cost of $38,000 to the estimated total depreciation value and then calculated a 30% tax credit, I found that this system's costs began somewhere around $74,000! Nearly double of an expected purchase price up front!

Should this client and that contract realize the full duration of its term, the client will have paid well over $57,000 in payments. To be completely fair, **without any issues involved,** even by paying $57,000+ for a 20 year period, this is still less than the expected utility costs for that same period for the same amount of kWh's. This is precisely how it is marketed, and this is where many people stop listening. All they hear is "much cheaper than the utility power" and they sign the bottom line of a 20 year contract.

I will end this section concerning a lease PPA with a question. What happens when the original lease company sells their contracts to someone else? Remember, with the 30% tax credit and all the depreciation value taken by the lease company within the first 5 years, they have recovered all their costs and have already made a very good profit by the 5th year.

This has been quite a chapter to write. I feel like I have delivered nothing but bad news within the confines of a lease arrangement. Even so, these are my true experiences and opinions. Let me end this chapter with a little bit of positive. The principle of a solar lease has its place. Those organizations that are tax exempt such as schools, churches, etc. cannot take advantage of the 30% Federal tax credit simply because they do not pay federal income tax. In these situations a lease is a good idea. The problems are not in the generic plan of a lease itself. The problems only show up due to the potential misuse and abuse by the creators and providers of our traditional solar leases that were born into existence from our "perfect storm" that occurred a few years ago. **There are very uncomfortable similarities between the rapid, lopsided growth of our current solar industry and the recent rise and fall of the mortgage industry.** Is history going to repeat itself so soon? I believe the potential is very likely. If so, the solar lease that was created in haste to push a new profit opportunity into a frenzy will be the culprit.

CHAPTER 5

The Community Group Business Plan

It is not an accident that this chapter follows the previous one. My reason is simple. The last chapter focused primarily on the misgivings and potential problems that await the current solar leases. This chapter will reveal how a solar lease could be honest, ethical and created on a foundation of integrity. A business relationship that has no hidden agendas and one in which all parties benefit.

Although this may seem a little unlikely in our modern times of "get what you can", I happen to know it is possible. How? Because I created such a plan. Along with my previous office manager, whom I have talked about often in this book, I put together a structure that had tremendous potential. I say "had" potential only because it never materialized. The reason it did not go anywhere was only a matter of organization. There were no ethical questions, no legal issues and definitely no abuse problems. The group of community leaders I spent several years working with were all volunteers. I personally hold each of them in the highest regard. They are good people. The simple fact was that they could never get to a point of organizing themselves properly. They remained in "volunteer mode". The roles of leadership were not established; therefore, we went in a continuous circle.

It was only a couple of years ago (2012) that Marlene and I presented this group with our completed plan. It was received very well. Some wanted to adopt it immediately. However, others were still wanting to research. By mid-2012 I could see the writing on the wall. They were only going to keep "researching" and not going to ever "act". With this awareness, I left them with my business plan and informed them to call me if they ever decided to actually engage it. They have not progressed at all since then. In fact, I believe they have basically dissolved. So even though I did not participate in the manifestation of this plan with this community group, I would like to share the nuts and bolts of how it was put together and what it would provide to all who would participate.

My purpose is simple. It belongs in this book. It shows a positive approach to a lease arrangement that is unlike any lease that is available today in the solar industry (at least in California). I believe I have done an adequate job revealing how and why our current leasing structures exist in the solar industry by using the "perfect solar storm" description in the previous chapters. Although this is how it is now, this is not how it has to be in the future. If a better alternative is not put forth and established very soon, the future of solar energy on a widespread basis in the private sector of this country is on very thin ice in my opinion.

The 12 Year Plan

When all of the traditional solar leases were exclusively doing 20-year terms, it was very disturbing to me that they promoted this as "the only way" to create a payment structure in which the client would see a monthly lease payment that did not exceed the offset utility cost amount they were accustomed to paying. In other words, the client was used to paying a certain utility cost each month, so the lease payment cannot exceed this same payment amount. I agreed with the principle, but disagreed with the length of the term (20 years). I strongly believe that the 20 year term was, and is, only for the benefit of the leasing company. They have a very big machine to feed. Remove a lot of that enormous cost overhead and greed and the term length is reduced drastically.

So I set out to prove this; and I did. On a side note, also keep in mind that as a very large buyer of solar products, it is likely that some of these mega companies are buying by the container full directly from the manufacturers. A typical container full of solar modules will equate to a quantity of approximately 600-800 modules. Therefore, it is also likely that these mega buyers pay less. I can personally tell you that their buying power, resulting in lower purchasing costs, is **not** passed on to the client. How do I know this? On many occasions I have had clients tell me that my gross system cost was less expensive than the leasing companies costs were, and usually the differences were significant.

Allow me to clarify by using an actual example with one of my clients. Late in 2013 one of my previous clients asked me to quote a system for a rental property he owned. For his own reasons, he includes the utility costs in the rent for his tenants. To install a solar system on a rental property can be a very good business decision. As the property owner and the one who was purchasing the solar, he receives the 30% tax credit and can depreciate the cost of the system after the tax credit is deducted, because the equipment was installed on a business for him. (A rental is actually a business to the property owner.) In order for the solar to offset approximately $4,000 of utility electric cost in the first year, I calculated a system that had a gross cost to him of a little over $33,000. Of this amount, he will receive just under $10,000 in a federal tax credit and then depreciate the remaining $23,000(+/-).

He had also acquired other quotes from two other companies. Both of these were big leasing companies from the Sacramento area. My client insisted upon showing me the **best one** of the other two. I usually do not care to see costs from anyone else, although when people are trying to compare, I like to see the equipment list so I can provide them with an accurate comparable. However, in this case he insisted I look at the other companies costs also. For their system, which was extremely close to the same size as mine, they were $41,000(+) in gross costs. We were both providing a completely installed system that included all the necessary paperwork. I will openly tell you that with my $33,000 system, I profited $6,000. This means that they were profiting $14,000! Also, it is fair to assume that they buy the equipment at a lessor cost than I do. On an additional side note, I had it completed within 6 weeks of my client's decision to proceed. The "mega company" was quoting a 3-6 month lead-time.

In the case of solar companies, bigger is definitely not better. By the time those big companies pay all the commissioned sales people, support all that office staff and pay for all those company vehicles running around, it is easy to understand their need to charge so much more. In any business that sells a product and/or service to the public, it is always the end user that ends up paying for all the overhead generated along the "food chain" of all those associated companies. The higher the overhead costs are within the product manufacturing company, the wholesale distribution company, the retail sales company and finally the installation company, the more the end user (client) pays. It is as simple as that. It is only with very convincing marketing and salesmanship talents that you, the client, become convinced that bigger is better when choosing a solar company.

Over the past 3-4 years, I have had multiple exposures such as the example I shared via this client. **In each case, their need to feed that hungry cost overhead machine revealed elevated costs.** There is **only one reason** the big leasing companies thrive: **monthly payments.** They totally focus their sales efforts on the monthly payment aspect of their deal. Next, they convince you of the long-term warranty that they proclaim. (We've already talked about this aspect in previous chapters). Due to our "perfect storm" situation that came together in the past decade, the approach used by these leasing companies was only going to succeed. Many clients feel "forced" to use this method because they have no other means to acquire an otherwise expensive item. I completely understand why this has occurred. However, just because all the ingredients came together to create such a situation, does not make it a good one. Each person must decide for themselves their own priorities. It is not my intent in this book to do that for any of you. It is strictly my purpose to give you "inside" information based on reality, experience and sincerity.

The Triple Win

I mentioned previously that I considered the 12 year business plan that I created for the community group to be a win-win-win situation. I'd like to share the basic ingredients of that plan to show how it performed for all three of the associated entities. First let's look at the "client" aspect of the 12 year plan. Most of the traditional leases offer "no money down". This may sound attractive, but I do not believe it is best. Any costs that are financed over time come with some type of attached additional expense, usually an interest charge. Also, I believe that when a client does not initially contribute, there is a lacking in the "sense of ownership" psychology. There can be a gap in the level of personal responsibility felt by someone who only agrees with something, but does not contribute to their decision monetarily. For both of these reasons, the 12 year plan required a 10% down payment. I will use a page directly from my plan to provide numbers as an analogy. These numbers would have been used in a real deal with a client needing this size of solar system. This is a roof mounted system on a residence located within the PG&E utility district of California. This system would offset an average of $1,400 in utility costs the first year.

- Gross system cost: $15,000 (completely installed)
- 10% Client deposit: $1,500
- Monthly lease payment: $112.93 (1st four years)
- Monthly lease payment increased by 2%/year for years 5-12
- 12 year total of all accumulative payments: $17,881
- Client final buyout payment: (10%) $1,500
- Total client expenditures: $20,881 (over 12 years)

This equates to a total finance charge on the original amount of $12,000 (after the initial deposit and final buyout of $3,000 collectively) of just $5,881 for all 12 years. This reveals an interest rate of approximately 5%. During the 12 year period, the average utility cost offset was approximately $23,658. I will also point out that it is likely that the inverter was also replaced by the groups "in-house" (local) warranty program **that is completely spelled out** in the agreement. With this 12 year plan, the client owned the system outright **with no hidden catch** at the end of 12 years. This is not clear at all within the traditional 20 year leasing programs. **Their contracts are very vague pertaining to the end result of who actually owns the equipment after 20 years.**

So from the clients perspective, a modest 10% deposit is paid, the total of all their payments is nearly $3,000 less than what the utility costs would have been, and they financed all of this at 5% (+/-) for 12 years. Also, the client did business face-to-face with the financing entity because they were the investors who lived in the same community. Everything is disclosed, nothing is illusive. Financially speaking, it is a very good deal to only pay 5% interest for a long-term (12 years) borrowing or lease option. Most interest bearing payment structures go up as the length of time increases due to the length of time the lender is exposed (at risk). 5% for 12 years is very attractive.

Now let's take a look from an investor's perspective. I did not set up this part of our plan with an intent to make the investors rich. However, a good rate of return is achieved with a somewhat low risk investment. Again, the borrowers (or clients) are their "neighbors" so to speak. The equipment is the collateral, and the client is very motivated to make the monthly payments for the simple fact that it offsets the same amount or more in their utility costs. **In 12 years they will own it debt**

free and realize many more years of "free power". The client is very likely to **not** default on our solar plan.

However, we do not live in a perfect world so I built in a protection device for the individual investor. A single investor did not fund a specific client. Instead, the investor put money into a structure that would be set up to act as a "pool" of all the funds. On the outside chance a client did default, the costs of that lost revenue were to be absorbed by the profit margins of this new entity. Also, a client did not qualify just because of the blanks they filled in on an application. Remember, this was to be a very localized face-to-face operation. A large part of a client's qualifications would be based on personal history in the local area. Here are precise numbers I took directly from a page in the 12 year plan. This is the "return table" for an investment of $25,000:

- Initial investment contribution: $25,000
- 30% Federal tax credit received: $7,500
- One-time finance charge received: $750
- 144 Monthly payments X $209.14: $30,116.16
- Total gross receipts for 12 years: $38,366.16
- Net return: $13,366.16

This equates to a 53% return on the initial investment over 12 years. This return percentage always stayed the same regardless of the investment amount. If the initial investment amount was $100,000 instead of $25,000, as we just examined, all of our numbers revealed above would be multiplied by 4. As I stated previously, this was not intended to make any investor wealthy. It is the "second link" in a chain of 3 parties whereas **all 3 benefitted.** I believe, and many others agreed, that this is an attractive, solid, reasonable opportunity for any investor who cared about what they accomplished with their money and not just their own profit margin.

Finally let's examine the third leg of the plan. This involved the coexistence of two entities that acted together. One of these was a group of policy makers and decision makers that acted as a board of directors. This group would be derived from members of the community who were directly involved in some capacity with this endeavor. A company would be formed with an established bank account, set of bylaws, etc. The second portion of this coexistence was the physically functioning part of the makeup. It is within this capacity that I fit in. This included the field labor, payroll, design and installation of the systems, etc. The relationship between myself and the community group entity was based on a 1099 scenario. I would act as the contractor and supply and install the equipment along with the hiring/firing of field employees. I would be in charge of scheduling and all the associated paperwork of a client's system.

In order for me to include in my 12-year plan a projection of business volume, I needed a platform from which to start. I asked some of the more involved community people what they thought was a reasonable starting point. They in turn asked me what I thought was a reasonable expectation of total systems that my company could install along with what my experience in this geographical area would support. After comparing all of our experiences and realistic expectations, we settled on one million dollars' worth of total system installs the first year. Much of my confidence came from one woman in particular who was a dominant player in this group. She has had many years of experience around community investments etc. She directed me to use one million dollars the first year as an investment platform. She seemed confident that if we did proceed into the manifestation of this endeavor, acquiring that amount was very reasonable.

So with a million dollars to work with, I put together a one year projection consisting of a variety of different sizes and applications of solar systems. Here are the basic numbers directly from a page in the 12 year plan.

- Total investor contributions (one year): $1,003,850
- Combined number of systems installed: 32
- Total system costs including client deposits: $1,144,000
- 12-year breakdown for these 32 systems as follows:
  - Total Client Costs: $1,585,216
  - Total Investor Income (Return): $1,541,327
  - Total Community Group Income: $376,494
  - Total Installation Contractor Income: $171,600

As you can see, the return to all the investors combined over 12 years revealed an increase of $537,477. The 32 different systems installed that first year ranged anywhere from a small $15,000 residential system to a much larger $80,000 commercial system. We would spread it around fairly between the residential customers and the local business owners.

Over the course of the 12 years, the community group as a unit made an estimated $90,697 in net profit after all projected expenses. The design and installation contractor (in this case it was me) was paid $171,600 all up front within the first year. This was to be paid as a schedule 1099. This amount reflects a gross profit prior to personal income tax. All other equipment and labor expenses have been previously accounted for.

In some ways it saddens me that this plan was not put into use. I believe that it could have genuinely benefitted all involved. I also believe that I have shown the basic ingredients of what a legitimate and ethical lease arrangement could look like within the solar industry. Unfortunately, the "large machines" require a much bigger diet of the end users hard earned finances. Although I have placed the general overall picture of my own 12 year plan in this book, which is protected by standard copyright laws, I encourage any of you who may have a local situation that could benefit from such an arrangement to pursue it. It would give me great pleasure to learn of a community that took some of these ideas and created their own "triple win".

If you do choose to build on my plan, I will ask one thing: You only do so with integrity and The Golden Rule as your foundation. Should you be tempted to create a plan in any other way, I would ask that you do not associate my name.

CHAPTER 6

My Opinions of Equipment

You know the old saying, "You can ask 10 different people what is best and you will get 10 different answers?" Typically this is true, however, your definition of what constitutes "best" is the determining factor in your opinion. So with that said, I will give you my definition of what "best" means to me in conjunction with solar products. Believe it or not, I can do this in just three words – least, history, and personally. I realize that together, these three words make no sense. So I will explain my meaning of each of these words, one at a time, along with what this means concerning solar products.

First, we have "least". To me this simply means a minimum. No bells and whistles, just a basic system. It has been my experience that the **least** technology involved with a functioning solar system; the more reliable it is long-term. Obviously, the solar components themselves represent advanced technology based on our human history. It is important you do not misunderstand what I am saying. I do not mean **no** technology, that would actually be an oxymoron. I mean unnecessary technology.

When people ask me a question like this one, "Do I need that in my system?", I first answer by emphasizing the word "need". If by "need" they mean "or else it will not come on and work", then I obviously answer, "Yes you will need that part." However, these days in the very confusing world of solar, the **impression** of "need" is greatly overused. One of the well-marketed "buzz-words" constantly thrown out by some salespeople is "efficiency". I cannot tell you how many people I come in contact with who have been completely sucked in by this illusion. I will make a statement now that would be something you would likely hear coming from certain salespeople who push an exclusive product brand. "My competitors only have 250 watt modules, but we have 300 watt modules!" Kind of like a car salesman might say, "Theirs is 250 horsepower, but ours is 300 horsepower!" Your first thought is probably "more power is good".

Let me break down the "more power" reality with the solar modules. To do so, I will first stay with the car analogy. If you were looking at two different new cars side-by-side and they cost the same, both looked good and had all of your desired equipment and they even got the same miles per gallon of gas, yet one of them had a 300 horsepower engine versus the other one's 250 horsepower engine, which one would you buy? Did any of you choose the smaller engine car? Probably not. Why? Because you believe you got more for the same cost.

Now watch what happens when I alter our above scenario slightly. Instead of buying a car as a single unit, what if you bought a car based on power output or production? In other words, a cars' cost is determined by horsepower. What if you had to pay $100 for every single horsepower rating of that car? The 250 horsepower car would cost $25,000 and the 300 horsepower car would cost $30,000. So now your choice is not so easy. The question becomes, how powerful do you need? So far this actually seems like a very good way to price a car doesn't it?

With all of the other components being the same, the only real decision is how big is "best" for **you.** But wait, there is a trick up the sleeves of some of the solar folks. When solar modules (which are by far the bulk of a systems total cost) are bought and/or sold, they are priced according to a "watt" of rated power. You may go on the internet right now and find a module outlet source that quotes the modules by the unit, but I will tell you this is only to make it simple for you, the public, to understand. Manufacturing and distribution all deal with solar modules on a cost per watt basis. Companies like mine buy our modules from our favorite wholesale distributors by the watt not by the each.

To cross-reference our car analogy, the wattage of solar modules is very much the same as the horsepower of a car. A single solar module is a combined collection of individual "cells" that makeup the particular modules' total wattage (or horsepower) rating. So now if we return to our different solar modules and their respective sizes, we would assume that if the cost per watt were the same, the larger wattage modules would cost more due to their larger wattage. If this were how it actually happened, I would consider this practice fair and acceptable. Remember, just a minute ago I said that some of the solar module manufacturers and salespeople have a trick up their sleeve. Well the trick I am referring to is centered on that overused word "efficiency". It is vital to your understanding of this discussion that you know, **when one solar module is more "efficient" than another is, it does not mean it is a better value.** Contrary, in some cases these salespeople use the overall increased efficiencies of their module to charge more per watt.

By now you are likely confused. I will clear it all up for you rather easily in this next statement. *Increased efficiency in relationship to a solar module **only means** that this module makes the same power in a smaller space.* For instance, a typical module is around 39 inches wide and 65 inches long. As I write this, this typical module will have a rating of 250 watts total. So now when another module can produce 280 watts within the same overall dimensions, it is achieved by having a more efficient method of assembling the module. Remember, **you buy solar by the watt not by the each.** The illusive marketing skills of some companies convince their clients that they get more power for their money with larger modules. The reality is that a client's system size is determined by wattage requirements not by quantity of solar modules. The "trick" is that by convincing the client that bigger is better, they can actually charge more per watt of power for their modules.

Consider this analogy. Your basis is a cost of $5 per watt of solar power. A 250 watt module will cost $1,250. Likewise, a 280 watt module will cost $1,400. This scenario is fair because the cost per watt is the same. But now the salesperson has convinced you that you are getting more bang for your buck with the 280 watt modules that encompass the same overall physical dimensions as the 250 watt module. This is achieved due to the "increased efficiencies" of the 280 watt module. You are told, with this increased efficiency factor you should expect to pay more per watt, right? Wrong. If your needs dictate a total system size of 5,000 watts of solar power, it does not matter if you use 20 of the 250 watt modules or 18 of the 280 watt modules. The complete overall wattage size of the system is roughly the same. So if you are going to pay for 5,000 watts of total solar power, why would you pay more per watt for 18 modules than you would for 20 modules?

The only time this should come into question is when the available space to place the modules is limited. **If room is not an issue, do not pay more per watt for your total solar system.** I have seen companies convince clients that their "more efficient" module is worth 15-20% more money. The life expectancy is the same. The manufacturer warranty is the same. The industry standard is something like one in 10,000 modules will go bad in the first few years. These days with the advanced robotics of manufacturing facilities, component assembly quality is very good. I have also heard arguments that a few less modules means less labor and mounting hardware. This is true; however, it is typically a case of "tripping over dollars to pick up dimes". The minor cost savings in labor and mounting hardware for those couple of fewer modules on an average system does not come close to offsetting the elevated costs in the modules. Make sure you understand this prior to deciding on a brand of module. If your available space is sufficient for your desired total system size, do not succumb to the "ours is more efficient so it costs more" sales pitch.

Now let's focus on the "central point" of all systems, the inverter(s). As described earlier, the inverter represents the "heartbeat" of a functioning system. Very much the same as a transmission in a car, this single component puts all the horsepower (wattage) together and makes it all work. The warranty on the inverter is typically 10 years, so it is very likely that this will be the component that will need to be replaced sometime during the life of your complete system. As mentioned very thoroughly earlier, I do not trust the longevity of most of the current big leasing companies along with their guarantee of 20 years that is attached to their 20-year contracts. However, in a relationship between a client and installer that is based on integrity; choose an inverter brand with a good, long history.

The reality is that none of them have much of a history here in the U.S., only because we are relatively new to the widespread use of solar in general.

With this being said, some of the inverter companies have very stable long histories in the European countries such as Germany. These are the ones I use and would strongly recommend to anyone. At this point, I am going to reintroduce our first key word this chapter is centered around, "least". In the past few years, we have had a few inverter companies show up here in America. It seems the latest thing is something called a "microinverter". As the name implies, these are much smaller than a standard "string inverter". Several years ago, a couple of my past employees were excited about using these. They were the latest and greatest technology! Along with all the claims of better performance, came an extended warranty timeframe of 20 years. So I agreed to try them for a few jobs. We probably installed somewhere between 200 and 300 of these things on multiple locations within a year or so. Again, this "advanced technology" was not "needed", but it is desired by many.

With just a 5 or 6-year history as of now (2014), I am still very skeptical of their value and reliability. Why? Because for the past 2 years we have been regularly going back to some of our installed locations and replacing some of them. I have not, and will not, install any more of these in the near future. Oh sure they are under warranty, at least for now as long as this company remains in business, but the $150 they pay me to go replace one is not even close to covering the cost, not to mention it is my reputation with the client that is attached to these things.

So once again, in the solar industry, it has been proven to me through my own experiences, that "extra, high tech" means tomorrow will likely bring problems with those unnecessary bells and whistles. Give me a straightforward "string inverter" with a long history in Germany and I will tell you that the odds are very good it will cause no problems until it begins to age between the 8-12 year mark. In their own right, the string inverters of German descent are a product of advanced technology, but they are tried and proven well beyond our own newly developed solar industry here in the U.S.

Before I move on, I should describe just what a microinverter is. You will recall that a string inverter is a single unit that manages a group of solar modules. With a microinverter, there is one of these very small units for every one or two modules. These inverters are only a couple of inches thick and less than one foot square in size. They are mounted directly under their respective module. This means when one of them goes out, you are up on the roof removing the entire module. If the array of modules happens to be moderately large and the bad inverter is out in the middle of the module array, it can take several hours to remove all of the necessary modules in front of your destination just to replace the bad one.

Also, as with our "more efficient" solar modules using the slightly smaller area they encompass as an excuse to charge more money, the microinverter system will nearly always cost more per watt than a comparably sized system with a string inverter. I will say that if these small units had a 20-year history of reliability as their string inverter cousins do, they would have a very good benefit in locations of partial sun and partial shade as the day wears on. But for now, at least for me, their quality and reliability is not good enough for me to attach my reputation to.

So now we have come to the last piece of the puzzle in which I am on the side of "least technology" (sometimes). This has to do with mounting procedures and specifically automated moving mounts, better known as "trackers". A tracker is a type of mount in which the modules are bolted to a framework that very slowly moves throughout the day in order to keep the modules in a direct facing of the sun. I have heard claims of increased production as much as 35% more over a stationary mounting situation. I believe this is somewhat exaggerated, but nevertheless, a solar module does indeed make the most power when it is clean, cool, and directly facing the sun. The issue is due to moving parts and the method by which it is "told" to move. Ask any machinist, mechanic, or farmer for that matter and they will tell you that when moving parts are introduced, the odds of failure rapidly increase. With the incredibly slow speed that trackers move, the issue of friction and wear is very minimal.

What does happen though is a malfunction in the automated part of what controls its movement. I have seen and repaired units in which a small controller that you could fit in your pocket went out and the entire assembly consisting of approximately 3,000 watts of solar power was stuck. Also, it seems as though they will usually stick in the early morning position. It returns to that position at the end of a day and remains there until the next morning, but as the sun moves it does not. If this goes unnoticed for several days, a large quantity of production can be lost. So with this, I am mixed on the use of trackers. If the available space is very limited, a tracker can maximize the solar production from the limited space that is available for your array. I would only suggest using a tracker under two conditions. One, the space is way too small for a "fixed" mounting procedure that will produce the desired amount of power. Two, there is routinely someone around to check on it. Do not put a tracker out in the "back forty" and go by to check it once a month.

Keep in mind, that as with anything that consists of more parts, the cost is higher. A tracker that holds 3,000 watts of solar power will cost considerably more than a simple fixed frame of the same size. The only time this will be a good investment is when the utility rate structure that is being offset with the solar production is quite high. Do not put a tracker on a solar system that is offsetting utility power that costs $.10 per kWh. It will never return its investment to you with such low utility rates.

Trackers can be a good idea if the space demands it, someone will keep a close eye on it, and it increases the solar power production sufficiently to offset the additional cost of high priced utility power fast enough to pay for itself in a reasonable timeframe. Do your own homework. Do the math before you decide. I have found that in the past few years the cost of modules has reduced so much that justifying the added cost of a tracker does not make sense. I simply advise my clients to buy a few more of the inexpensive modules and stay with a fixed mount that will not ever wear out or malfunction. All of this of course, is assuming that space is not limited.

At the beginning of this chapter, I listed three words that define what I believe constitutes "best". We have just spent considerable time on the first one which was "least". With this word, as you have seen, I am referring to "least technology". You may recall that the second word is "history". I have actually already covered this during our discussions in this chapter on inverters. To me, "history" means tried and proven. We all live with technology that once was new. For some people, the "drive" is very strong to have whatever is the "latest and greatest". This psychological effect is generated from an elevated level of competition. They must belong to the first group that has...

At the personal level, I can understand this trait, although

I do not possess it myself. If I encounter such a person as a potential client, the odds are fairly good they will not become my client. The old saying "the customer is always right", does not apply in my book, when I understand the components much better than they do and it is my reputation that is accompanying those components. Unfortunately, many companies will simply nod their head in agreement with anything the client says in order to get the sale. I will not do so. Although it is rare, I have encountered a few people who went on the internet or talked to another company first and got their first impressions of what is "best" from an incompetent source. Then I come along and basically disagree. Even though I am as tactful and polite as I can be, it can sometimes be close to impossible to change first impressions.

If you are getting multiple stories from different people concerning what is best for **you** with regards to solar power, ask yourself two questions. What is their history? Ask for referrals, many of them. I provide a page full of typed names and phone numbers of past clients. Next, and more importantly, ask yourself if what they are telling you is best for **you** or for **them.** They should be able to provide a long history of success for both themselves **and** the equipment they use. Research the companies of the inverters and modules they are proposing. Do they only offer one? Do you have choices in the equipment? Do they know **your** personal property and power needs or are you just the next appointment? Are you a "custom" project for them or just the next "same thing"? Tell them to close their laptop for a while and look at you and talk to you. You would be surprised how many salespeople have simply memorized a routine presentation. Take them out of their routine and they do not know what to say or do. I do not own a laptop. I walk into someone's house or office and go over a very complete, written quote package that typically takes 2-3 minutes. Then I leave it there for them to keep and I tell them that I would prefer to answer their questions. We will sit there, face-to-face, **without any electronics** and talk.

If I am not coming to them via a referral or they do not know me, I will openly offer my history. I will tell them precisely why I conduct my solar business the way I do and precisely why I use the equipment I do. If they ask for equipment choices, such as American made versus Chinese made, I tell them that will not be a problem. I reveal any cost differences that may apply. Integrity is really all there is to it.

The third word I listed is "personally". I am very often asked, "Do you do the work personally?" I tell them that I have three employees who will do a lot of it, but I will be directly involved also. In my mid fifties, I do not wish to run around on a lot of steep roofs anymore or dig a lot of trenches. However, I am always personally involved. Sometimes I stay at the jobsite all day, other times I will come and go depending on what stage the installation is at. My two guys are very competent and honest. I do not need to babysit them. I have an office manager who does all the paperwork. With the mega solar companies, what do you suppose the odds are of the owner being personally involved on your project?

In closing this chapter, I will remind all of you that "bigger" is definitely not better when it comes to which company you choose for your system. I strongly encourage all of you in the market to obtain solar for your own use, to sincerely understand the information throughout this book. I am very confident that you are reading things in these pages that you have not, and probably will not, hear anywhere else. The only thing I have to sell you is this book itself. Obviously you have already made the decision to buy it. Now my only purpose is to provide you the tools you need to wade through all the confusion, misrepresentation, and incompetence that have engulfed this industry. If the wonderful benefits that the equipment can provide are to continue to be sought after in a few years, a balance needs to occur in this industry. Currently we are out of balance in how this industry is presented to the public.

CHAPTER 7

The "Business" of Solar

Are you considering a career in the solar industry? If so, at which capacity are you the most interested? Also, very importantly, are you listening to the best advice concerning your potential new direction? Although this chapter will focus on the business side of this industry, there will be valuable information for those of you contemplating becoming a client and obtaining the products for your own use also. My experience has been within the position of dealing with the public. I have over 30 years of this type of capacity involving multiple businesses as an owner-operator. For those of you interested in research and/or manufacturing, I am simply not your guy.

At this point I will give you your first bit of advice. Each time you ask someone what **you** should do, consider two things very seriously as you absorb their responses. One, what is their personal history in the area in which they are offering you their opinions and two, what do they have to personally gain from your potential decision? Next, before you go any further, **clearly** and **completely** define what **your** definition of success is. In the American business culture of our current times, it seems that most people would have a large income level be the number one priority in their definition of success. If this is the only thing on your mind, I suggest you either reconsider your personal priority structure or make sure that you have a "backup" plan for when you find yourself looking for a new career in a few years.

There are two general categories of income potential in the solar industry at the design and installation levels. The first is short-term and the second is long-term. If your primary goal is a large income right now, I can nearly assure you that your career will be short-term. To become busy enough and large enough to sustain an uninterrupted flow of clients at the end-user level, makes it extremely likely that you would need to conform to the current methods that have been adopted by the "main stream" of solar providers and installers. In short, you have jumped on the proverbial bandwagon.

The "bubble" will probably continue for a few more years at most. Now that I have made such bold, confident statements, you are no doubt asking yourself how do I know this? The truth is, I do not absolutely know how the future will play out, but I will give you my reasons as to why I am so confident. It starts with a general psychology of business in this country. I suggest that in every circumstance in which an industry is still alive **and well** in 30-40 years after it is conceived in the general public eye, there was/is a foundation of "principle" and "reputation concerns" at its beginning. As the solar industry is portrayed currently in the public arena, this type of foundation is not apparent. For those of you who believe that the solar industry is all about the "green" aspects of helping our planet, I am sorry to say that you are very naïve. I can absolutely tell you that if solar does not provide a good return on investment for the end-user monetarily speaking, this industry stops. The problem we currently have is within the ability of the financing mechanisms in the solar arena to convince the public that due to the portrayed guarantees made by the "bankers", everything will end "happily ever after".

The public does not want to hear what is looming in the future because they want to believe it is a good thing to use solar. For many people, the reality is that they can't buy it outright. So, if your attraction toward the solar industry as a career is founded in making a good income immediately, you can likely achieve that (for a few years). However if you value your personal reputation and are motivated to have a long career in the solar arena, you must be willing to openly examine the current trend and where it is leading this industry. Remember the age-old philosophy: "Look at what the masses are doing and then do the opposite." This generic philosophy is only referring to long-term decisions. **In the short-term, "riding the wave" will produce today's income but leave you looking for a new job tomorrow.**

With all of this now being said, there are good opportunities for those of you who have the priority structure that dictates a long-term approach. I would like to share with those of you in this category, my experiences and opinions based on several decades of business experience, along with what is working for me to produce success (as I define it) in the solar industry. First and foremost, I do not attach myself to anything or anyone who is only focusing on making money. Do not misunderstand; I do desire a good income and I do achieve this, but it is only on my terms. "Following the crowd" is not part of my makeup.

You can absolutely achieve a solid solar business at the design and installation level if you are in it for the long haul. On average, it takes 3-5 years to build a "name" and reputation for yourself. Contrary, this can be destroyed nearly overnight. **Always** apply The Golden Rule. Treat your clients the same as you want to be treated by those you do business with when you are the client. If you take advantage of your clients, do not complain when the auto mechanic does the same to you (hypothetically speaking). The only truly successful companies long-term are achieved and sustained based on a positive reputation and referrals. "Wave riders" are not truly successful long-term, because as we all know, the wave eventually hits the wall (the shore).

Also, you must align yourself with others who operate in the same philosophy as you. You will recall my story about Andrew earlier in this book. I have aligned myself with him and his company, long-term, precisely because he conducts himself very much the same as I do. Next, if you are an employee working for a solar installer, be very aware of his/her personal reputation. Their decisions and portrayal have a direct impact on you and your career. If your employer is so large that you do not know who the owner(s) is/are, you are likely not going to have a long future in this industry (at least at the installation level). If this represents your current position, you should really contemplate your future and have a strategy for your career ready should you need to make a change. If you are, or plan on becoming self-employed, all the same priorities apply. Only hire and hold on to employees who possess integrity. These people are directly in view of your clients and impact your reputation greatly.

Be very careful when hiring so-called experienced employees. In my exposures of having hundreds of employees over the years, this can equate to previous bad habits. With standards such as I have, an employee who comes to me boasting about having 10 or 20 years in another company structure, usually causes me concern. Although I am very interested in people who are comfortable with my line of work, I do not wish to inherit a mentality of lower standards than I require. I have found it is much easier to teach someone my ways, without first attempting to overcome previous impressions of how they may have been misled. The bottom line is simple. The people you associate with professionally (and personally for that matter) have a tremendous impact on **your** reputation.

Branding

For those of you unfamiliar with the term "branding", as it relates to business, please allow me to provide a brief description. This typically refers to aligning yourself with certain products. If you are "branded" with XYZ Product, you are many times an exclusive user of their product line. If you only promote a single brand of product in your business and you purchase a reasonable quantity on a regular basis, many times this company will give you incentives to continue. This is very common in retail business today. They may help pay for advertising, provide cost breaks, or even offer occasional promotional packages. With industries operating in long, well-established arenas, it can be a good idea for a small company to align themselves with a tried and proven product line that enjoys a strong reputation. When it comes to the solar industry however, I will say that if I were (and I haven't) to ever **exclusively** align myself with any single product, it would only be an inverter company, and that company would have roots well beyond the newly established solar industry in the U.S.

For those of you who believe this would be wise with a module company, please reconsider. There will be a lot of mergers within module companies in the not-so-far-off future. For the next 5 years (at least) keep your options open as to which module(s) you use. Whatever you do, do not succumb to the high-priced "efficiency" claims of better quality. I do not use the "most efficient" modules on the market today. They are not a good value for my clients. I choose module brands by looking at the company's strength. There are many brands available, and they are all extremely close in their manufacturing methods. The warranties are the same, even though some try to manipulate the wording to give the impression theirs is better. A warranty is only as good as the company's strength and longevity. As with the leasing structure, you can be promised anything, but if the company ceases to exist, their promises go away with them. So use a brand of modules that has a strong company behind it.

In the business of solar, change is a common occurrence. Stay flexible in your module brand choices. If you completely align yourself with a single module brand, put logos of this brand on your truck, etc., and in a couple of years that brand disappears, you now must start over and reinvent yourself in the public eye. Do not give away the control of your business to a "brand" of individuals that you do not know.

Racking and Mounting

This is a part of the solar system that quite honestly does not interest the average client. Again, there are many good mounting products out there that are of good quality. In fact, they are so similar, that these companies have a difficult time showing how theirs may be better. So in an attempt to show superiority over a competitor, some of them will focus on the difficulty (or lack there of) with the installation of their products.

This one makes me laugh. A group of designers in a lab are

deciding how many hours it takes to install their product on a typical location. You will hear claims such as "lessen your installation time by 20%" or "a moderate decrease in labor costs with our product". These are silly, vague claims to say the least. When it comes to which mounting methods you adopt, use commonsense. Which types fit **your** operation? Which brands are readily available, a good value, and are widely accepted by the engineering standards in your geographical area? Answer these questions to choose your racking type and brand.

Companies that build the racking and mounting components have very little, if any actual experience in applying their products in "real world" scenarios. A mockup of an installation in a controlled environment is not even close to a good test. If you have any mechanical savvy at all, and you better if you are going to install solar, you will quickly identify your favorite brand(s).

Responsibilities

In my opinion, retail and/or service companies go too far these days. I am not referring to the actual product or physical service they provide, I am referring to entering in an area that should be the clients' responsibility. Our culture has created a very "detached" way of doing business. In an attempt to make it extremely easy for clients to participate in whatever it is they are selling, many businesses do **everything** for the client. The recent mortgage disaster revealed this in a huge way. Homeowners were literally "created" by the financers of that past widespread debacle. It didn't matter if you could actually handle the mortgage, you were approved. All the steps were done for you. Just "sign here" and here are the keys to your new house!

The solar lease is a "first cousin" to that same mentality. I strongly encourage any of you, whether your position is that of designer/installer or client, to do your part. Do it with integrity and require the others involved to do their part. If you are in the position of installer, it should not be your responsibility to figure out how your client will pay for it. Your responsibility is an ethical portrayal of yourself and your company, quality employees, a quality installation, and a product you truly believe in. Accomplish this in a timely manner and you are done. Your clients' responsibility is paying for it, providing you access and a working environment as agreed upon, and honestly reflecting their experiences to those they talk to.

This is how business should be conducted in my opinion. Unfortunately, the practices of many in the solar industry reflect a much different approach. Should you come across a lending institution that offers solar financing on a "purchase" basis, talk to them personally before you refer them. Tell them you will ask for feedback from everyone you send their way. Once you have decided to refer them, be very clear and upfront with that first person you tell about this lender. Let them know that this is a new lender you have no experience with and would greatly appreciate their opinions of service quality once they have gained exposure to them. If you receive positive feedback and continue referring this lender, **only** pass on the contact info. Do not become involved in the private affairs of the client. Do not call the lender in advance and attempt to vouch for a client. Simply put the two parties together and stand aside. Make sure both parties are familiar with the terms of payment your contract stipulates with your client. Misunderstandings in communicating the details cause a large portion of any hard feelings that may occur. Apply The Golden Rule of communication. Talk to everyone the same as you wish to be talked to.

Clear, concise, and open communication is an absolute key to your success.

Attaching to the Grid

The vast majority of all solar installations are attached to the local source of utility "grid" service. With these types of installations, the purpose of the solar equipment is to coexist with the utility. The produced solar power does not provide direct power to isolated loads exclusively at any given time. The solar power is constantly changing. Time of day, clouds, seasons of the year, even the cleanliness of the modules all dictate production performance. When your lights are on and the refrigerator, air conditioner, and/or laundry machines are running, they require a much more stable and consistent flow of power than a solar system without a storage component such as batteries can provide.

So the purpose of this type of solar system is simply to "put back" the used power you have drawn from the grid. The grid is readily available 24/7 as you need it (with the exception of breakdowns). The produced solar power is obviously confined to daylight hours and all sorts of conditions that have a direct effect on its performance. To conduct an installation business in today's solar industry will almost assuredly require you to attach your installed systems to the grid. If your company is going to provide a "turn key" service to your clients, you need to provide the final step in the complete functionality of a solar system that coexists with the utility company.

There is a procedure that each utility has to accept the incoming privately generated solar power into their grid system. Becoming proficient in this procedure will be vital to your operation. If you do not have an office person or the desire to do this yourself, you can hire people to do this for your as a "sub contractor". If you choose this route, **be very careful** who you select. Until your client is approved by the local utility company, they cannot receive credit for their produced solar power. You may have done an excellent installation job and performed extremely well within the physical part of the project, but if it takes months and months to complete the utility approved connection part of the transaction, your client will not be happy and **your** reputation is damaged. Any time you hand over a portion of the control of a project, you should know exactly who you are dealing with. They directly affect you.

Permits and Building Departments

I will devote the next chapter to an experience my company recently had with a specific building department. So drastic was this experience that I will use an entire chapter to expose the details. However, to finish up our discussion here, I will talk about the permitting procedure in conjunction with typical solar installs. When performing installations "for hire", you must be a licensed contractor. Contractors licenses are issued by the state and each state will have a list of the approved categories that can install solar systems. The building jurisdictions are locally responsible for issuing the permits, performing the inspections, and adhering to the various codes that are applicable. As a business owner, you do not personally have to be a licensed contractor, however, you will need to employ someone who is.

In California, a person applying to get a contractors license must have 8,000 hours of experience in the field they are applying for and the combined total of these 8,000 hours must occur within a 10-year time span. Do you also know that a typical building inspector can have very minimal training when hired?

Seems a little backwards doesn't it? Nevertheless, if you install solar as a business you need a proper license. Also, I encourage you to have liability insurance with a minimum of one million dollars in coverage. I have found that the typical homeowner does not require, or even know to ask the contractor about liability insurance. However, nearly every commercial installation will have that business owner requiring such insurance from anyone who works on their property. Likewise, if you have employees, have workers compensation insurance. If you are hiring employees "under the table" and they get hurt, it will be a very bad experience for everyone involved. Why would you even consider risking your business and reputation, not to mention the exposure to your clients and employees by not having workers compensation insurance?

Believe me when I tell you that I have had those few employees who were lacking in integrity and ethics and who abused me and the system. I have watched the political system here in California grant completely bogus claims to a few of the problematic past employees I briefly had. Even so, I will not risk myself and my company for a few dollars.

Again, speaking from a long-term perspective, as a solar installer that has a priority of a good reputation, you will find that most building departments are fairly user friendly. Considering several decades of experience, dozens of building jurisdictions, dozens of individual inspectors, and a wide variety of permit types, I have had minimal issues with negative experiences with building departments in general. I can easily say that during those few instances where there were conflicts, ego was the primary cause. Beyond this, the most common source of disagreement between inspectors and contractors will come due to different impressions and/or perspectives of any given code. Over the years, I have had minimal such occurrences.

CHAPTER 8

An Uncommon Abuse

This is a chapter that I have been contemplating for several months. It is not pleasant, yet I believe it is necessary. My struggles in presenting this chapter have not been a question of should I include it in this book, but rather how I would deliver the content. Before I begin the actual content of this story, I would like to spend some time explaining a little preliminary information. It is with all my sincerity that I express to all of you this story is true. I will disclose everything with only an honest portrayal. There is no exaggeration and no "ad-lib" information involved. The actual experiences contained throughout this story happened in mid-2014, which is only a few months ago as I write this. My memory is very fresh and as you will come to realize, this is not an easily forgettable experience.

My personal struggle in how I would expose this content has been an ongoing internal affair. As you are aware, this is chapter 8. The first 7 chapters were easy to produce, however, when I finally came to this place in the book, I felt an urge to pause. With the aid of exterior distractions that have shown up at just the right time (as they will do if you "listen"), I delayed putting pen to paper toward this chapter for nearly a week. Then, yesterday as I was driving, it cleared up. I felt a new direction that I was completely at ease in pursuing. So now I am at peace with myself on how this content will be exposed. I will say that my priority with all of my books is to help. With this particular book, I am using my years of exposure to the solar industry, with my 30+ years of experience in working with the public, in an attempt to reveal truths that are not being told or felt yet. I was preparing to write this book prior to the timeframe in which this story took place. With this awareness, it was easier for me to deal with the actual happenings as they unfolded.

Honesty dictates that I reveal to all of you my intentions. Up until yesterday, they were to expose the entity involved. A part of me truly wants vindication, however, there is a bigger purpose to this book than my personal revenge. On many occasions in the past couple of months, I envisioned myself delivering a copy of this completed book to all of the predominant individuals that occupy high-level positions within this city. With a smile on my face, I was going to personally hand deliver copies to the three individuals that were at the center of this experience first, then I was going to work my way up. The Community Development Director, the City Manager, the Mayor's Office and finally each and every city council member. I was even going to provide copies to the Chamber of Commerce to pass out to their members. This exercise would have probably brought me a temporary feeling of vindication, but I have a bigger purpose.

I truly hope that this story will cause an increase in the pursuit of integrity in all of those cities and counties that are exposed to this book. As you will soon come to know, I have made a decision to not work within this city again. The level of human behavior I encountered during this recent experience was extremely inappropriate. There were three foundational ingredients that created this ordeal – dishonesty, incompetence, and ego. I personally can deal with modest egos and I have patience with a certain amount of ignorance if the individual is sincere. Intentional dishonesty is not something I will associate with. Abusive liars are not the type of human being I will share space with under any circumstances.

This story involved the City of Woodland, California building department. As I have shown thus far in this book, a building department is one of the primary factors in solar installations. As I attempt to recall all the different city and county building jurisdictions I have obtained permits from and completed a wide variety of jobs in, I realize it is more than I can recall. Encompassing the entire northern half of California for several decades, I have shaken the hands of dozens of inspectors. Although there have been those occasional conflicts, in each and every case the issue was quickly worked out with little felt impact. But, within the actions of this particular city's building department, a much different outcome was to be.

It should be known that I have been personally and professionally involved with this city for over 25 years. With many construction projects and solar installations being successfully accomplished by my company for many years in this city, this recent experience came as a complete surprise (at first). So now, as we traverse this story together, I wish to remind you, these are all actual events. No exaggerations or misrepresentations have ever, or will ever, find their way into my books. Should you choose to believe otherwise, you will be mistaken.

I have a suggestion that may seem a little odd, but does serve a purpose. I suggest you have a note pad handy and "keep score". Every time we come to a place in which you believe misconduct or inappropriate behavior is displayed, make a mark on your note pad. (Yes, there will be that many.) I am going to do the same. At the end of this chapter, I will reveal how many marks I have on my "score card". As we begin, contemplate this question, who gives the "cop" a ticket?

This Really Happened

Someone I have known for a while called me one day in the spring of this year (2014). She told me her parents were interested in solar for their home and wanted to talk to me. I have met her parents previously on a couple of occasions and found them very pleasant. Her dad, which I will refer to as "Mr. Client", was recently retired from a long career. Her mom, "Mrs. Client" was still at her position at a well-known financial institution and was planning on retiring in a couple of years. This couple represents a very common type of client for me. At or near retirement and capable of purchasing the equipment. I met with them and provided them with detailed cost quotes and return-on-investment analysis for two systems. There was a mid-level system and a large system that would essentially replace nearly all of their annual utility electric costs.

After a few days of our meeting, they informed me that they wished to proceed with the large system. So my office manager and I created the necessary paperwork to obtain the permit. A contract was put into place and my field foreman submitted our permit package to the city building department. We were issued the permit the following day. The official title of the man who approved our permit package (as was done many times before) is *"Senior Building Plans Examiner"*. An impressive title that suggests experience and knowledge.

This system was not complicated, at least not by my standards, and I did not expect any issues. This house had a partial single level along with a partial second level in which we were using roof space on both levels. It is quite common with many building jurisdictions to have only a "final inspection" upon completion of a roof-mounted solar array. Such is the case in this city. So, within three weeks of our initial cost and system proposals, the installation was completed. (By the way, your scorecard should still be empty.) My field foreman scheduled the final inspection and waited for the inspector all morning. Some jurisdictions will provide an A.M. or P.M. timeframe, others will even get to within a two-hour window; however, this one does not provide either (at least with us). So, I pay my guy $25/hour to wait.

If you are wondering why I do not do this myself, I will explain. For many years I was present at every inspection. As we became focused with solar installations, I found a reoccurring redundancy with the inspections. Approximately three years ago, I began having my field foreman perform this task. It has been my practice for the past 10 years or so, to have my key people be more involved in the routine exposures of permits and inspections. This has worked very well and in fact, has worked very well in this **same city with the same inspector** on many occasions.

An important side note that will show itself as we proceed through this story is that until this job, it had been approximately 1½ years since our last job in this city. Sometimes it simply goes like that. I had in no way been avoiding this city, I had just simply found all of our jobs during this 1½ years elsewhere. Well over 90% of my work now comes via personal referrals. I do not engage a continuous advertising campaign. Sometimes I receive multiple calls from a certain geographical area in a short timeframe. During this past couple of years, we have spent a lot of time completing jobs in the surrounding rural areas. With all of this past experience, I had no concerns about continuing this method.

Now I will share the official title of the man who performed the inspection, *"Senior Building Inspector"*. Again, this title suggests experience and knowledge. On the day of the inspection, as I have just explained, I was not personally present. My field foreman, **whom I've known for 23 years** was representing our company. Also present was Mr. Client. An extremely important fact is that Mr. Client remained inside the house with the windows open due to the very nice weather. Upon his arrival, the inspector was **unaware that Mr. Client could hear the communications between himself and my foreman.** My foreman was standing inside the garage with the big car door open. We had installed a subpanel on the inside portion of the garage wall. *(To continue with this story and remain complete and authentic, I must involve a certain amount of language and technical terms that some of you may not understand. To aid with your understanding, I've provided a glossary in the back of this book).*

As the inspector walked toward my foreman he asked for the "plans". When issued a permit, one of the copies of the plans is stamped: "Approved, Field Copy". The contractor provides this copy to the inspector during inspections. As he took our field set of plans and began to look at them, he noticed the new subpanel on the wall in front of him. He quickly realized that this new subpanel was rated 200 amps. He then learned that the original main service panel on the house was rated at 100 amps. His demeanor and tone then became very harsh and rude. His comments were obviously against our methods and when he saw that the **"approved"** plans supported our method, he quickly complained about his peer who approved those plans. He suggested they did not know what they were doing in the office. His tone became increasingly harsh and insulting. Comments such as, "I don't have time for this!", "You can't do this!", and "This isn't right!" I used exclamation points to emphasize his attitude. Remember, he is unaware that Mr. Client can hear much of this.

He and my foreman then walked around the garage wall to the exterior part of the same wall. We had installed our inverters there for ease of wiring and to locate the inverters in an inconspicuous place. There were 3 individual "string" inverters rated at a maximum of 4000 watts each. I specifically designed the system as such to provide the most efficient power production. We had placed a small array of modules on 3 different portions of the roof. These roof sections received sunlight differently during the day. Therefore, I used 3 little inverters instead of one or two larger inverts to accommodate the different roof sections. Each inverter managed a single portion of the roof to maximize its production. The usage of three small inverters obviously perplexed the inspector. His comments suggested he had not ever seen three inverters on a house. Things like "nobody does this!" were said. It also appeared that the usage of three inverters was supporting his previous disagreement with the larger subpanel being used that was rated for a higher amperage than was the main service panel.

Please understand that it is not only the content of his words that should be impacting your "score card", but rather his very harsh and insulting tone and delivery. This is very hard for me to translate. This is the "energy" that accompanies all face-to-face communications. With this being said, as I will show later, there is an obvious lack of knowledge he is exposing via his comments. He did not understand what he was looking at in terms of electrical applications in this case. Remember my comment in a previous chapter? To apply for a contractor's license, one must have a minimum of 8000 hours, which is essentially 4 years of full-time experience in the field they are applying for within a time span of 10 years. To apply for a building inspector's job, no field experience is required and very little previous training is needed. Does this seem like a good idea? Is this balanced?

At this point my foreman was questioning him as to any codes that prevent what we had done. He could not provide any. (Now we must begin to allow for his ego.) After his initial reactions and rudeness, it seemed very unlikely he would do any research in an attempt to find the actual answer. However, he then stopped and called the office to talk to the man who approved the plans. They spent 15-20 minutes on the phone. Again no answers were derived. So at this point **he decided to make it our problem.** I will now print for you two lines from a "correction notice" he wrote concerning the subpanel issue. These words are **exactly** as he wrote them.

1. "Provide load calcs. from an electrical engineer or licensed electrical contractor".
2. "Ran 200 amp subpanel from 100 main panel".

By this time it was obvious that we were going to fail the inspection; (which is extremely rare for us). So in an attempt to only go through a re-inspection once, my foreman asked him if he would go on the roof to see if all was ok up there before he left. He did, and also found issues there. I later conceded to several corrections pertaining to those issues and we made the necessary changes to accommodate those corrections. As you will soon see, I sent a letter to the inspector, the plans examiner and also to their immediate supervisor addressing the events of that inspection day. Contained in this letter were my explanations as to why we did our installation in this manner, along with my responses to the other issues which we did in fact change. The official title of their supervisor is *"Chief Building Official"*. Although I doubted some of those other small corrections were necessary, I could see it both ways and chose to show compromise on my part.

During the inspector's time on the roof with my foreman, Mr. Client was upstairs in his house with the windows open. It became increasingly obvious that this inspector was not happy at all. Additional sarcastic comments kept coming from him. Things like "I should have been here 10 minutes!" "I don't have time for this!" Finally he departed leaving behind a "correction notice sheet" containing a total of seven items. Of these 7, the final two were the lines I quoted earlier. The other 5 items, I addressed in my letter to all three of the city employees I've mentioned and we made the changes in the field. Here is an exact copy of that letter. I have hidden the names intentionally.

Letter To:
Chief Building Official
Senior Building Plans Examiner
Senior Building Inspector

Joe Gwerder
General Building Contractor – Lic #765818
Specializing in Rural Construction
Residential – Farm – Ranch
30+ Years Experience

"Solar with Integrity"
Backup power during outages
Remote water pumping
Utility bill reduction or elimination
Residential – Business – Agriculture

May 8, 2014

To Whom It May Concern, and Specifically XXXX – City of Woodland Building Inspector:

Hello XXXX,

My name is Joe Gwerder. I am a general contractor, as you may know, and my companies are Constant Energy Source and Custom Design and Construction. On Monday, May 5, 2014, you performed an inspection at my job site located at XXXX Street in XXXX. This was for a solar (photovoltaic) final inspection. My field foreman was present and representing our company. Also present, although indirectly, was the homeowner which is also our client. I refer to our client as having an indirect presence because he primarily overheard most of the conversation between you and my employee via open windows. In a moment I will respond to each of the seven comments you wrote on a "correction notice" which you then provided a copy of to my employee. However, I would first like to address something I consider much more important considering your professional position. Also, I will briefly elaborate on my professional positions along with a few personal opinions.

It was revealed to me that your presentation was abrupt, rude, insulting and lacked an easy to understand language usage. The homeowner, who stated to me he has no personal knowledge of you, was extremely unappreciative of your verbal displays to my employee. He felt you were rude and delivered your verbal communications in a "scolding" manner. My employee was left very confused and also in total disagreement with your tone and demeanor. He said you "talked in circles and did not provide clear descriptions of your perspective on several items".

While I do not wish to debate with you on what was said and/or how it was said, I will make several generic suggestions to you. As humans our communications have little do with the actual content of the words. It is widely believed among many psychologists that only approximately 15% of our total value in our communications are the words. The vast majority of our communication impact is found in tone, body language, physical gestures, volume fluctuations, etc. I suggest if you were to honestly examine these aspects of your presentation you may be surprised at your discovery. Of course this will only be beneficial if you can **sincerely** and **honestly** open yourself up to this type of personal examination.

It seems apparent you are frustrated and I'll bet angry much of the time. Presenting yourself outwardly with an abrupt, angry delivery does indeed accomplish several things (none of them good). You are engulfing yourself in very damaging levels of stress. Stress is quite harmful mentally, emotionally and physically. Why would you choose to be this way? It is **your choice** to be like that. To place blame elsewhere completely shows an absence of personal responsibility.

Joe Gwerder
General Building Contractor – Lic #765818
Specializing in Rural Construction
Residential – Farm – Ranch
30+ Years Experience

"Solar with Integrity"
Backup power during outages
Remote water pumping
Utility bill reduction or elimination
Residential – Business - Agriculture

Next, the recipients of your disposition do not respect you or this type of conduct. Respect is earned not demanded. I believe you are a very experienced and knowledgeable individual who could be of great benefit to your profession. However, when you present yourself in a manner that does not reflect The Golden Rule, you have only caused damage to yourself and to those who are participants. Calm is the one who is confident.

I also believe you routinely assume the position of competing with us – the contractors. We are on the same team. Regardless of what you may otherwise think, it is **our** reputation at stake. Most clients never even know the inspector's name. Personally, I am a Yolo County native with a 30+ year career in the construction field. Although I have done a fair amount of construction and solar work within the City of Woodland, I have done the majority of my jobs in the rural regions of the counties from Redding to Madera. I have personally known my employee, that was present at the above mentioned job site, for over 20 years. He has been in the construction industry focusing primarily on residential electrical and plumbing along with framing for 15 years. Regardless of the level of knowledge or experience anyone has whom you come in contact with professionally, your highest level of calm, respectful, professional conduct should always be first and foremost.

If you truly wish to improve your state of happiness, search for the root causes of your frustrations. They will not be found on the roof tops of job sites. It will be a much more personal search. In closing this portion of my communication with you, I will say that I realize you have likely never been "spoken" to like this before, especially from someone in the construction world so-to-speak. I ask that you sincerely consider what I have said in this note. I have not intended any sarcasm and I am completely sincere in my approach. There is much more to me than you would guess.

Thank you for your time.

Joe Gwerder

Joe Gwerder
General Building Contractor – Lic #765818
Specializing in Rural Construction
Residential – Farm – Ranch
30+ Years Experience

"Solar with Integrity"
Backup power during outages
Remote water pumping
Utility bill reduction or elimination
Residential – Business - Agriculture

Responses to 7 "Correction" Items

1) In 2010 I was contacted by the training officer from Woodland Fire Department. He had a request for me to provide safety training to the Woodland fire personnel concerning solar applications on roof tops in which they may need to deal with a structure fire. I agreed and did a 2 hour session for each of the 3 shifts at the XXXX station. I had an enclosed trailer in those days that was fully setup as an actual equipment classroom. There were modules on the roof along with all the other equipment mounted on the walls inside the trailer. I did not have any wiring connected to the modules in order to ensure safety. During these six hours I spent with them we talked about the current egress requirements and what was expected in the near future. At that time it was my understanding that the periodic 3' egress aisles applied after a length of 50 lin ft of an array was reached. This meant that nearly every S.F.R. would not be subject due to the typical array size was less than 50' in length on nearly all houses. Since 2010 I have neglected to update my knowledge of the situation. It does make logical sense to have the ridge area open on one side for fire venting purposes. I am in agreement with this correction request and upon reinspection you will find that 8 of the solar modules have been relocated to a portion of the 1st floor roof thus making all the roof areas accessible as described.

2) We have used these labels on hundreds of locations in many different climate areas. It is my understanding that we comply with the label design requirements using red coloring with white lettering, etc. I agree that this batch seemed to have much less adhesive value than we are accustomed to. Upon reinspection you will find new labels with an additional wrapping of clear plastic tape to ensure adhesion to the conduit.

3) As described in item #1, eight modules on the 2nd floor roof have been removed thus exposing this plumbing vent.

4) We were not aware that metallic pull boxes required bonding if they were not containing splices and all the wire was insulated. This is specifically why we used a plastic junction box on the roof where there are splices contained within and this is also where the bare bond wire terminates. Upon reinspection you will find a grounding lug has been attached to the metallic pull boxes on the inside and the ground wire is attached to this lug.

5) (It is difficult to read this writing on the correction card at #5). I believe your comments state that a typical ground bus within a panel is not good enough due to the use of screws within this bus. Also, I think you are referring to the ground splice within the plastic junction box on the roof. Upon reinspection you will find a heavy crimped clamp in all the above mentioned locations. If this was not your intent, more legible writing would be appreciated.

6) I do not agree with this request for several reasons:
   a. There were no additional loads applied to the newly installed sub panel. We simply removed all the existing loads from the existing 125 amp main panel (100 amp continuous) and reinstalled them on new, same size O.C.P.D.'s in the new 200 amp sub panel.

Joe Gwerder
General Building Contractor – Lic #765818
Specializing in Rural Construction
Residential – Farm – Ranch
30+ Years Experience

"Solar with Integrity"
Backup power during outages
Remote water pumping
Utility bill reduction or elimination
Residential – Business - Agriculture

---

b. Apparently you made it clear to my employee your opinions of a general contractor
    installing solar. I only have 2 comments toward this. First, you may be surprised how many
    C-10 electricians have questioned me on the applications and functions of a solar system.
    It is naïve to believe that any given license classification guarantees expertise. I can tell
    you that in my travels I have come in contact with many inspectors in dozens of
    jurisdictions and the lack of consistency in your profession is very frustrating. The obvious
    point is in your stereotyping. Next, the State of California has determined that my
    classification of a contractors license is valid and completely sufficient with regards to a
    solar energy system design and installation (see attached letter). I do not believe that the
    state would approve of local jurisdictions and/or individual inspectors deciding for
    themselves which license classifications are allowed to perform any given type of work.
c. Before moving on to #7, I feel I must be completely clear on the "load" aspect of this, or
    any, installation. For anyone such as yourself who has been exposed to electrical
    applications for many years you have only associated an O.C.P.D. as a load bearing device.
    This has been primarily true and it is easy to understand the conditioning everyone has
    been exposed to in this regard. However, it is very important that you can understand and
    accept that an O.C.P.D. attached to the A.C. side of an inverter **is not** a load. It is a **power
    production** O.C.P.D. **only.** Current flowing through an O.C.P.D. from the A.C. side of a solar
    inverter **only sends** power toward the loads and/or grid. At no time does the O.C.P.D.
    draw power from the grid. A load **only draws** power from a source. The solar system
    relates to the loads very much the same as the grid. Please see attached illustrations to
    clarify. In addition, we added the 200 amp sub panel as means to increase the available
    bus bar "stress" allotment. I do realize that with a Class B license I cannot **only** add sub
    panels. In this case it is a required and reasonable approach to the needed increase in bus
    bar size. As our plans show, a total of 45 amps in O.C.P.D.'s for the inverters were
    necessary. Even if we were to have taken the much more costly and time consuming route
    of increasing the main utility service to a 200 amp, we would only have had the 20%
    overage in bus bar rating available to us, which is 40 amps on a 200 amp panel. For all
    these reasons I believe this added 200 amp sub panel is absolutely a part of the total solar
    installation. As a service to our client, we moved the existing loads into our new panel
    with new individual O.C.P.D.'s that are of the very same size as were the old O.C.P.D.'s. No
    additional loads were added. The 200 amp O.C.P.D. in the new sub panel is completely
    irrelevant. It is supplied by a 100 amp O.C.P.D. located in the original main service panel.
    Regardless of how many or how large the O.C.P.D.'s are beyond the main service O.C.P.D.,
    it is within the max. capacity of the main service O.C.P.D. that all others are limited to. A
    basic understanding of current directional flow does not allow any other conclusions
    beyond the path of travel outlined above. As inspectors you are involved with this type of
    situation routinely. I challenge you to find very many main panels or sub panels in which
    the combined total ratings of all the load O.C.P.D.'s do not add up to well more than the

Joe Gwerder
General Building Contractor – Lic #765818
Specializing in Rural Construction
Residential – Farm – Ranch
30+ Years Experience

"Solar with Integrity"
Backup power during outages
Remote water pumping
Utility bill reduction or elimination
Residential – Business - Agriculture

---

panel rating or the main supply O.C.P.D. rating itself. This is because it does not matter what the sizes of the O.C.P.D.'s are beyond the main service O.C.P.D. All other O.C.P.D.'s are subordinate to the main supply O.C.P.D. If this remains beyond your comprehension, as a gesture of good will, we will remove or bypass the 200 amp O.C.P.D. in the subpanel and attach by using another 100 amp O.C.P.D. or by using lugs. This maneuver will not change the function nor will it provide any added benefit, however I am willing to accommodate as a means of completion.

7) I believe I have fully explained this inaccurate correction request above. Actually, this is not written as a correction at all. You simply stated what we did.

We will request a reinspection soon.

Thank You,

Joe Gwerder

CC: XXXX – Building Inspector
   XXXX – Building Plans Examiner
   XXXX – Chief Building Official
   XXXX – Client

dayTime- Solar on
EXAMPLE #1

Grid and Solar in Conjunction

dayTime- Solar on
EXAMPLE #2

Night Time- Solar off
EXAMPLE #3

Loads
(50 AMPS)

Loads
(30 AMPS)

Loads
20 AMPS

30 AMPS

20 AMPS

20 AMPS

20 AMPS

Solar
(30 AMPS)

Solar
(30 AMPS)

10 AMPS

Solar
(30 AMPS)
(idle)

Grid
(100 AMP
MAIN)

Grid
(100 AMP
MAIN)

Grid
(100 AMP
MAIN)

As I believe most of you will agree, I did not deliver my letter in a rude or insulting manner. I also intentionally left out a few of the additional comments made by "Mr. Client" concerning the inspector's behavior. They were not flattering to say the least. At this point I would like to add a brief description of my foreman, whom I've known for 23 years as I write this. He is in his mid-forties and possesses an extremely mild manner. I have **not once** seen him angry to the point of losing his cool. Exaggeration is absolutely not his style. I have trusted his evaluations for a very long time. When I combined his descriptions along with the additional evaluations of Mr. Client, I was completely convinced that the happenings, as described above, were, and are, very accurate. I am willing to bet, that when they each read this this segment, they will tell me that I was too kind in my descriptions of the inspector's behavior that day. (So how does your score card look so far?)

Believe me, this was the easy part. What is left to come, will have many of you believing that certain job dismissals are in order. I will say, that all three of the recipients of my letter would not wear any uniform that associated them with me or my company.

Making it up as They Go

The above letter was hand delivered on a Thursday to the front counter person at this building department. She responded very politely that "all three of these guys are at work today, so they will each get it". This was Thursday a.m. By Monday afternoon we had not gotten any responses, so I asked my foreman to schedule the re-inspection for the next day (Tuesday). He did so and intended to be at the jobsite Tuesday morning to wait for the inspector. At approximately 7 am Tuesday, my foreman received a call directly from the inspector stating he would not re-inspect that day because we had not addressed items 6 and 7 on the correction notice. Again, his attitude was not pleasant. With zero responses in 3 business days to my letter, I thought it might be over. I was drastically mistaken!

Now I was very insulted and realized that we were dealing with very childish behavior from this department. At this point, I'd like to pose a question. How many of you would have expected the Chief Building Official to become involved? Ya, me too. Not a peep. Unless the young lady at the counter was wrong (his office is just around the corner) he got my letter Thursday prior. Not wanting to play these types of ego driven childish games, I decided to exercise one of the options the inspector wrote on the correction notice. You remember: "An Electrical Engineer **or** a Licensed Electrical Contractor".

Knowing that our installation method concerning the 200 amp subpanel was correct, I chose the least expensive route first – an electrical contractor.

Even though this would represent an unjustified expense, due to the building department's lack of understanding, I wanted this whole thing to end. I know many electricians in the area, but chose a guy I've known for years. His dad is a retired electrician. He has his own license and worked with his dad for 15 years until he retired. Now he runs his own business. Also, I know that his work is very familiar to this building department. Upon my call, he was happy to help. I met him at the job site and told him our dilemma. He looked at what was done and commented very favorably with several compliments. He said he would call the inspector to see what it was that they wanted in a letter from him to accommodate their requirements. I told him the problem was a lack of understanding by the officials of how "loads" and "supplies" function in an electrical panel. His comment was, "I don't know why they can't get that?" I then asked him if the inspector had been possessing a worsening attitude lately. He said that a lot of guys have trouble with him.

During this process, I made two other phone calls for informational purposes. You will simply have to take my word about the integrity of both of these two men whom I called as this was unfolding. I would trust both of them with anything I have. They are both honest and very truthful men of character. One is a general contractor as I am. The other is a retired building inspector. I have known and worked with both of them for many years. You may recall that I had not done any work in this town for 1½ years prior to this job, however, my good friend and general contractor has routinely worked there. Positively aware of his integrity, I knew I could count on his evaluations of that building department recently. He told me that this inspector was "losing it". He said that "he is not making any friends. He shows up unannounced and looks for things someone is doing wrong." His comments went on and he told me that he was not surprised by my recent experience.

Next, I spoke to the retired inspector. This man spent the last 5 or 6 years prior to his retirement in this same building department. He worked directly with all three officials in question here. To sum up his comments, he very much disliked working with them but wanted to complete those few remaining years of service prior to retiring. His words were the most direct toward the Chief Building Official. He said "he was not to be trusted" and was a "snake". His comments toward the plans examiner were directed toward his "incompetence". Finally the description he offered about the inspector was founded in a "bad attitude". Given my recent experiences, I completely believe and agree with both of their personal opinions towards the three building department employees we have discussed.

Now, returning to my electrician who was going to call the inspector and proclaim his agreement with my methods. He didn't get through to him. He only got a voicemail. Next he called the plans examiner in the office. This man answered and informed the electrician that "**they**" have decided that "**they**" will now only accept an electrical engineer as a means to decide. So amongst themselves, without notice to me, the option written on the correction notice was withdrawn. **It is my firm belief that they knew they were wrong and had a dominating egotistical inspector calling the shots, with his boss nowhere to be found. The plans examiner made it a habit during this entire ordeal to say one thing today and**

something else tomorrow. He does not have enough knowledge to do his job and is afraid of the overbearing disposition of the inspector in my opinion. So now, without any choice at all, I contacted an electrical engineer. Before I disclose the happenings with the engineer, how is your score card coming along so far?

Unbelieveable!

Upon my call to this engineer, I made an appointment to talk to the owner the following afternoon. I drove the 30 minutes to his office in West Sacramento. I prefer face-to-face meetings when possible and I wanted to provide him a copy and also review with him my "single line drawing" in which the city **approved** as part of my permit package. Note: A single line drawing simply shows all the major components and the path of travel in an electrical configuration. We spent a little over 30 minutes together then he made a copy of my drawing and said he would have a letter for me in a day or two. He wanted to also discuss my methods with his vice president of the company to ensure their agreement. As you will see in the following letter, **they absolutely agreed** with our installation methods. Here now is an exact copy of the letter provided to me by this electrical engineering firm. Again, I have hidden the names. Also included here, you will see an exact copy of the single line drawing that I created and the engineer refers to. On a side note: The reference within this letter pertaining to "CEC" stands for "California Electric Code". Please understand that the actual drawing used for the permit was much larger and drawn very neatly.

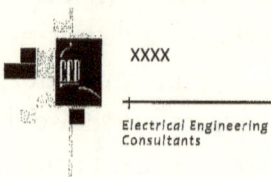

XXXX

Electrical Engineering
Consultants

XXXX
President
XXXX
Vice President

Joe Gwerder
XXXX

May 19, 2014

Subject: Explanation of CEC 705.12 (D) Compliance for single family residence.

Dear Joe,

CEC 705.12(D) is addressing the connection of utility power fed thru the main breaker panel and PV power fed thru the load side of the same panel. Assuming the panel main breaker and the bus bar have the same current rating there could be a remote possibility when you have power fed thru both the utility and the PV and at the same instant of time the load demand is higher than the breaker max specification the breaker will not trip because the additional power is coming from the PV and cause the panel bus bar to work beyond its maximum specification and fail.

On this residence the following change has been done to remedy the situation as depicted on the attached one line diagram:
A new 200A bus bar has been added and it is a buffer between the utility 100A panel and the Solar panel, if we do a CEC 705.12D analysis as on the previous paragraph we observe that if we have both the utility and PV sources feeding the new 200A bus bar sub-panel and the load demand at that instant of time exceed the 100A, it will comply with CEC 705.12(D). There is no possibility the 100A main service panel bus bar will ever go beyond the max specification. Assuming a trip point of 80A for the utility main breaker and 12A for each of the solar panel breaker the maximum current possible of 116A flowing thru the new 200A panel. On the unlikely event you allow for 120% of the breakers rating you will have a maximum of 174A thru the 200A bus bar sub-panel. As demonstrated above the 100A breaker will normally trip as required, the PV solar panel Breakers will trip as normally required, the 100A bus bar on the utility panel will never Exceed its maximum rating and the new 200A bus bar sub panel will be able to meet the specification of CEC 705.12(D).

I have attached a paper that will help to understand the intent of CEC 705.12 (D).

If you should have any questions please contact our office.

Respectfully,

XXXX
President

XXXX
Vice President

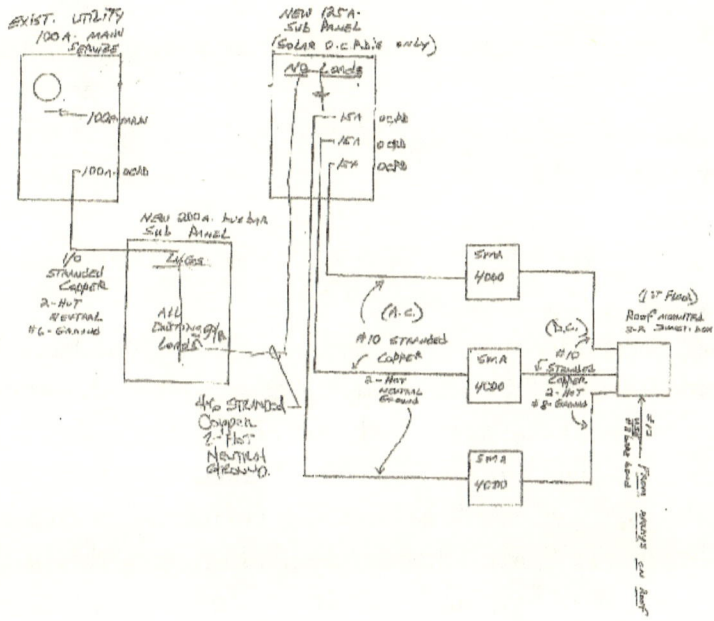

Upon receipt of this letter, I had my foreman hand deliver a copy to the building department. Again, the nice young lady at the counter assured him that the plans examiner would receive it. On a side note, when my foreman went in to the building department, he specifically asked to see the plans examiner. The counter person went to go get him. She returned and asked what this was in reference to. After informing her of the nature of his business, she once again disappeared. Upon her reappearance she informed my foreman that the plans examiner was "unavailable". For the next few days we were ignored once again. By now Mr. Client was very agitated. This childish delay was costing all of us very valuable time and a lot of money.

I made a suggestion to Mr. Client. I told him that I believed they were going to continue to avoid us. **It was now extremely obvious they have been completely incorrect in**

their stance on the subpanel issue and were now facing total embarrassment. I suggested that a strong complaint from a "citizen" would carry a lot more weight than from a contractor. (Inspectors tend to cater to the homeowners and compete with the contractors.) When this happens, you will find an inspector who lacks confidence. This was obviously the case. So Mr. Client began making angry phone calls. He connected with the community development director, who is the supervisor to the Chief Building Official, who has yet to become involved (at least openly). Again, another day goes by with nothing. Finally, in total frustration, Mr. Client called the city manager's office, but when asked the nature of his call, the manager was "unavailable". Then a day or two later, the director calls Mr. Client and tells him that "this will all be taken care of by 5pm today. If it is not, you call me back directly".

Well guess what? It wasn't. By now we have seen 3 weeks pass since the initial inspection. Mr. Client informed the plans examiner that a letter was being drafted to send to the city council. This caused **some** movement. The plans examiner, who was obviously continuing to stall, said he was attempting to contact the engineer directly. He wanted to talk to him about the letter. Maybe they thought I forged it? Anything is possible with this group. Now, a certain "warning label" was all of a sudden a priority. This label is not part of the standard labels we typically apply so it had to be specially made. Again more delays. We created this label and **called the plans examiner to confirm its applied location. He said twice on the phone to "put it on the new subpanel we installed".** He also requested from the engineer that this label be "called out" in his letter. The engineer accommodated the building department on their request. The building department requested his letter be **sent directly to them.** I did not receive a copy. That is why the engineer's letter I included above is void of this label reference. **The plans examiner assured Mr. Client and my foreman that this label would suffice and everything else was good.**

So, finally after nearly a month of completely unnecessary delays and hardship, we scheduled a re-inspection. I specifically asked Mr. Client to be visibly present during the inspection. So, on inspection day as Mr. Client and my foreman awaited his arrival, the inspector does not show up. Instead, the building official comes himself. The first thing he found was the newly required label. **He insistently said it was on the wrong panel. "It should be on the original main panel outside".** My foreman, in disbelief, told him that "......(examiner) in your office told me to put it there! I even double checked and was told to put it there again!" It didn't matter, this was wrong. Then the building official looked at other things and made a completely new "corrections notice" list. My foreman directly said to him that **"the inspector requested those things this way".** Mr. Client then jumped in and suggested to the building official that they were running us around in circles. "You tell them one thing and your inspector tells them something different."

Nevertheless, their systematic game continued. (By the way, what are you up to on your score card now?) As the building official drove away, my foreman called me. To be perfectly clear on my continued absence during these encounters I will openly tell you I cannot handle this type of abusive human behavior. I do not trust my ability to stay calm and keep from saying things I may regret. My writing is my strength, so I stay with this. For those of you who believe that the old fashioned way of "yelling" and "verbal threats" would have been in order during this ordeal, I can and do completely understand. However, that is not my way. With my foreman's phone call to me explaining what just took place, I drove to the job site and met with him and Mr. Client. It was during this meeting that Mr. Client made a suggestion that I did not wish to believe.

Now What?

Remember the question I asked at the beginning of this chapter? It was, "Who gives the cop a ticket?" Who inspects the inspector's? Oh, the suggestion from Mr. Client, "They will never pass this. They want you out. Another solar company has them in their back pocket." Even with as much as we had been through, I really had a hard time believing this may be the case. Upon the departure of the building official, he stated he would email us the list of corrections "tomorrow". Didn't happen. Big surprise. Not knowing what to do next, we were all speechless. This experience is beyond words. A day later, Mr. Client called the building official to inquire about the promised email containing the new corrections. They would not communicate with my foreman or me at all. The email was finally sent containing a new group of corrections.

My foreman and I planned on performing these minor changes within two days in one last attempt to be done with this. I had to locate a specific item they now wanted. The local electrical supply house (which is a nationwide chain) does not stock this item. Real popular item wouldn't you say? The day before we were to show up and make the changes, Mr. Client called me. He said he has some information that I should know before I did anything else. **The Chief Building Official**

showed up at his house unannounced at approximately 2pm that day. He was invited in and sat in the front room. Mr. Client was distracted as his 93 year old mother who had just gotten out of the hospital was staying with them to recuperate. He and his sister were tending to her when the doorbell rang **unexpectedly,** and the building official was standing there. Mr. Client informed the official that he was busy and to give him a few minutes.

When they finally spoke, the building official made some very disturbing statements. **"Their work is so subpar that we don't know if we will ever pass it. We haven't called the state license board yet, but may do so."** *So now you should all be sitting down for this next statement.* **"You really should call Solar City. They spend half of their time fixing other people's problems." WOW! The city building official shows up at a client's door unannounced and, off-the-record, directly recommends a single company!** This other company, by the way, happens to be a huge leasing company that for the past couple of years has been installing all of the public schools and many other locations in town. Is any of this even close to appropriate behavior? Are there any conflicts here? When Mr. Client told me this on the phone, I was in shock. Was he right? Is the building official "on-the-take"? I thanked Mr. Client and said I needed to "be with it" for a while. I would be in touch in a couple of days or so.

My Plan

It is hard to describe what I went through for the next 2 days. I was hurt to the core. For those of you who have read my previous books, you know of my life's path. There has been a lot of personal struggle, but this one took its toll on me. We have all heard many stories of abuse and conspiracy in our current world, but as the saying goes, until it happens to you, you can't imagine how it feels. My reputation and professional record is one of extreme integrity. I do not know how to intentionally hurt anyone, but these people were portraying me as someone who is incompetent. **The opposite of the truth.** I jumped through all their made up hoops and still they couldn't' prove me wrong, so they turned to an **abuse that is cowardly and deceitful.**

As I always do these days, I took some "neutral" time to "listen". On the second day, I came to understand what I wanted to do. I was at peace with my new plan, so I called Mr. Client and asked to stop by and reveal it to him. Twenty minutes later I was sitting in his garage with him. No one else was present. Before I began, I asked him to hear me out before he responded. I had a feeling he might object, so I told him I was truly O.K. with what I was going to suggest. He agreed to hear all of my plan before he commented. I began by telling him that we must identify our objectives and pursue those objectives in a way that has the best chance of success. I listed only two objectives.

1. Realize a completion to this situation.
2. Do this in a way that allows him to keep the installed solar system on his house.

With this, he looked very curious and continued to restrain any comments. Then I made a very blunt statement," "Befriend the building official." I said for him to "portray the victim". I told him to "throw me under the bus". He was to go to the building official and act like a victim in this whole thing. Ask the official to help him finish this. Tell him that I was told to step aside and let someone else get it "passed". Tell him that you appreciated his visit the other day and want to know what to do next. I told Mr. Client that I would forfeit the remaining balance owed on the system of a little over $6,500. This would give him the resources to pay the city's "company of choice" to get it passed. As I revealed the details of this plan, Mr. Client looked very bothered. As I expected, he did not approve. He said this was completely wrong. He would not "throw me under the bus".

I responded with gratitude for his genuine concern for me and for pursing an ethical outcome, but insisted that this was the only way to achieve our objectives. I finally convinced him to play along, however, there were a few compromises. He said he would **call** the official. He really did not want to be in his presence. He refused to portray me as insufficient, so he would simply ask for help from the official without mentioning me. If I came up, he would tell the official that we had worked it out. I assured him this would work. I told him "they will not fail their own referral". I knew that their elevated egos were driving them and that this plan played directly into those illusive egos. Also, I know that the human being will go to great lengths to avoid a fear. They were afraid of me, their own incompetency, and exposure.

So the plan was put into motion. Mr. Client called the official and professed his desire for help. The building official jumped right in with both feet. He told Mr. Client to come down to his office right away and they would get this going. By the time Mr. Client arrived a few minutes later, **the official had already called Solar City.** But, wouldn't you know, they only work on **their equipment.** Remember the lie about ½ of their work……anyway, not to worry, another company **received a call from the official** on behalf of Mr. Client. (You don't think the craziness stops here do you? Oh no!) The boss of the "other company" was **taught the solar business by me!** That's right, and he did not leave my company on good terms. I'll just say that the title of this book is not part of his priority structure. He is an "everybody does it" kind of guy who jumped on the short-term bandwagon. The company he now manages has a priority of getting people "hooked" on solar. It is of no surprise to me that he would receive a personal call from the type of individual that this city building official obviously is. So now, even though this job was yet to be passed by the building department, I began to feel as though I was personally done with it.

On another side note, **my company "pulled" and paid for this permit based on my plans. I did not ever sign anything relinquishing this permit to anyone else.** In essence they stole it. This permit continued, and was eventually passed, via another company without my written permission. **A building permit is an "owned" legal document.** All of you lawyers out there think this is O.K.? This building department was simply doing whatever they wanted as they went.

Upon my belief that I was personally finished with this situation, I had my office manager type a letter that I drafted, addressed to the city council members and the mayor's office. I told her not to send it until Mr. Client had received an approved final inspection. Although he did eventually receive the approved final inspection, just as my plan was designed to accomplish, I actually did not ever send this final letter. Even though it has not been seen by the city officials (yet), I wish to include a copy of it here. Again, this is an **exact copy with the names hidden.**

Joe Gwerder
General Building Contractor – Lic #765818
Specializing in Rural Construction
Residential – Farm – Ranch
30+ Years Experience

"Solar with Integrity"
Backup power during outages
Remote water pumping
Utility bill reduction or elimination
Residential – Business – Agriculture

May 29, 2014

Woodland City Council Members
Mayor's Office

To Whom It May Concern (It should concern everyone):

My name is Joe Gwerder. I am a Yolo County native of 55 years. I have been a business owner for 26 years. A recent experience has caused a decision that I wish to inform you of. I am no longer going to conduct my business within the City of Woodland. The amount of ego, incompetence, and dishonesty that has encompassed my experience with one of your department's is beyond words.

As elected officials, I would like to believe your approach is more professional. I will admit I'm not very confident in receiving any inquiries from any of you. However, should you like to learn more of my story, I will provide you the details. I feel I should disclose that my recent experience, which was shared by my clients and employees, will become public knowledge as part of a book I will publish later this year.

I'll leave you with a quote from myself that highly resembles the conduct of several city employees:
    "When ego and ignorance combine, a troubled experience awaits."

I am truly disappointed.

Joe Gwerder

Owner: Constant Energy Source
    Custom Design & Construction

Author: *Listen Without Your Ears*
    Listen Out Loud
    20/20 Listening (Currently in Publishing Process)
    Solar Integrity (Coming in Late 2014)

As this unsent letter states, I will not conduct my business in this city any longer, or at least as long as the city employees involved remain. I refuse to willfully subject myself to his type of human interaction. Before I move on to a few closing comments pertaining to this chapter, it is time to tally up the score card. I have **fifteen** different circumstances of **misconduct** and **improper behavior** by one or more of these city employees. In my opinion, the majority of them are grounds for dismissal (especially concerning the Chief Building Official). I must also point out that as I wrote this story, I had several occasions in which I remembered additional happenings and statements made by the city folks that I did not go back and include. Otherwise I have presented the main points of this ordeal to the best of my memory. I expect that when my foreman and Mr. Client read this chapter, they will remind me of even more behaviors and/or statements of dishonesty and/or incompetence revealed by the city employees as it was happening.

In closing this chapter, I would like to acknowledge two extremely important people in my life. My fiancée Tracy and my son Matt. Not only are they family, they are my best friends. A father could not be closer to his adult son than I am with Matt. Likewise, I could not have a better partner and soon-to-be spouse than Tracy. The 6 weeks or so that I was engulfed in this experience, were also extremely hard on both of them. They lived through this injustice with me. Knowing my priorities of integrity, made this occurrence something they could barely accept. I am truly sorry they had to experience this event. Although they did not always agree with my approach, they supported my decisions with a level of strength that really helped me.

Also, I suggested very early in this chapter that I was going to deliver copies of this book to predominant people within this city. Currently I have decided to refrain from this action. As you can now realize, my temptation toward exposure and vindication is very strong, however, there is a bigger purpose. It is beyond obvious that this building department needs a drastic change. I do not wish to evoke my undue "bad press" on other departments within this city that have actual standards of integrity (assuming such departments exist). But, I do feel a responsibility to make known this department's misgivings, so as to aid in any improvements that are so desperately necessary.

With this in mind, I will personally deliver a draft copy of this book to the city manager in a private manner. I will inform him that this chapter is a true story based on his own city. Depending on the feelings I get when this time comes, will determine my decisions to be made toward any future action on my part. I would like to believe that this city manager will take action to improve his city's building department. (Talking is not action.) My personal circumstance does not require that I do any future jobs in this city. However, if I simply walk away silently, their egos and incompetence may (probably will) harm others in the future who intimidate them as I unintentionally have.

I really do not know if the Chief Building Official, or any other city employees, are guilty of showing favoritism to any specific company(s). Actually, I must retract that last statement. The Chief Building Official obviously favors two other companies. He made that perfectly clear by first, **personally referring them** and second, by **actually calling them himself** on behalf of a client. **My client.** What I meant to say was I do not know if any city employees are being directly compensated in some way to provide their favors. Isn't the simple fact that we are considering such a circumstance to have a reasonable chance of being true troubling enough on its own?

I'll leave you all with a few questions. If any one, or all of these three individuals worked for you, what would you do? How about if you worked with them as your peers and you were aware of their conduct, how would you react? Talk to them directly? Report it? Keep quiet?

What would Mr. or Mrs. Integrity do?

CHAPTER 9

The Top Ten

Although I have not intended for this book to be a "how to" book, I want to include the most common questions I receive along with honest answers and my opinions. By providing these within the confines of a book, you are not influenced by a salesperson who may (probably does) have a motivation to sell you something. I will do my best to be all inclusive and cover as many topics as I can in an attempt to leave you very informed. For those of you interested in a detailed explanation of the physics of solar (photovoltaic), I will suggest you find other sources to provide you with those details. It is not my objective to teach you how solar works, in a technical manner. My purpose is to give you a clear understanding of the basic function and benefits associated with the private usage of these products. When all parties involved operate with integrity, the benefits can be tremendous!

FAQ's, Answers, and Opinions

1. How much does an "average" system cost?

My initial short answer is actually with another question. How much does an average car cost? What this is saying is, there are more details needed to supply an answer that is remotely close to accurate for you. So with this, let's identify a few of the necessary details. To do so, I will create a hypothetical client: A residential system within the PG&E utility district of Northern California. Two adults in the house with monthly utility electric costs averaging $200. This would suggest wintertime costs of approximately $100 per month and summertime costs of approximately $300 per month. With this baseline we have an annual total of $2,400 in utility electric costs. The PG&E rate structure for residential customers is set up on a "tier" system. Generally speaking each tier has an allotted amount of kilowatt hours (kWh) in it during any billing cycle (one month +/-). As you consume the allotted kWh's in your first tier, you then advance to the next level which is higher in its cost/kWh. This process continues when and if you consume the total allotted kWh's within each tier in a given billing cycle. To properly determine a solar system size, we examine two things financially speaking.

1. The annual KWH's consumed, and
2. The total annual cost of these kWh's within a tiered structure.

A system's produced kWh's can be much more valuable to larger consumers. If you do not have "used" kWh's in the higher tiers during that month, your utility costs are reduced considerably. With this understanding it is easy to realize the function of a solar system that works in conjunction with the grid. Simply put, **the main function of the system is to provide some or all of the used KWH's to your account with the utility.** Due to the changing seasons and the typical metering laws pertaining to utility/solar interactive applications, the assessment of a needed system size is based on an annual analysis. Prior to solar, your relationship with your utility is basically monthly. After you have solar, your relationship becomes yearly.

So with our hypothetical home described above, I will tell you that based on my experience, this home is consuming approximately 8,000 – 9,000 kWh's annually. Now, I will also tell you that in an area of moderate sunshine such as Central and Northern California, a solar system size of approximately 5,000 watts (A.C.) would be very close to eliminating their utility electric costs annually. With this estimated size and assuming an easily installable location is present, this homeowner should expect to pay a gross cost of approximately $20,000 for their completely installed system. These costs are based on the summer of 2014 conditions in the solar market. Also, assuming this homeowner is a Federal income tax payer, they would be eligible to receive 30% of the $20,000 in a Federal tax credit as of 2014. After the $6,000 tax credit is realized, the remaining investment amount is $14,000. By inserting the $14,000 figure into a flow chart that begins with the utility savings for the first year being approximately $2,400 and using a calculation for future years that reflects the average inflation rate of the utility costs in their rate structure, this homeowner should expect a return on their investment within 5 years or so.

2. What are the warranties?

Beginning with the modules, which are the most expensive components as a whole in a functioning system, a 25-year warranty is standard. This warranty is not simply a guarantee that they will work for 25 years, but it is actually based on a certain level of operation. When you read the language in the many different versions of all the various manufacturers, you will find multiple ways they approach the **implied** warranty. Many of them attempt to manipulate the language for illusive reasons. The basic truth is that modules gradually weaken over the years. The premise of all the warranties on solar modules is that a loss of approximately eight tenths of one percent (.8%) is reasonable for each year they are exposed to the elements. With this, you will find nearly all of the module warranties calling out an **80% value at the 25-year mark.** So essentially, you can expect to lose up to 20% of power output of any given module by the time it is 25 years old and exposed to the outdoors.

Be careful of the illusive attempts by some to reconfigure the same warranty timeframe. I'll explain. If you look closely at the language of many of the listed warranties, you will find the timeframe divided into two "landmark" spots. The first will be at the 10-year mark and the second will be at 25 years as described above. Many will say that their modules will have a minimum output of 90% at the 10-year mark and then go on to say that this will be at least 80% at the 25-year mark. If this is where they stopped with their claim, all would be good. Instead, many companies will attempt an illusion with the aid of a visual graph. In this graph it **appears** as though their competitor's product loses 10% immediately and then stays at 90% for the first 10 years. It is very important that you remember the basic premise of a given modules' warranty and the actual rate of degradation that takes place. **Modules gradually get**

weaker. I will use the graph below to help illustrate. This graph is very similar to how many of the manufacturers portray their products and a close version of what you will see on many of their own specification documents (spec sheets).

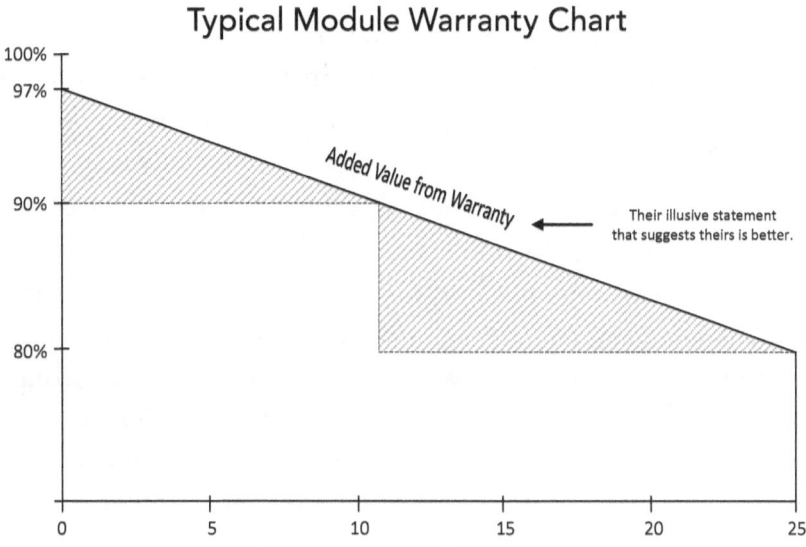

It is standard practice for most module manufacturers to begin with 97% after the first year of exposure. The lower portion of the graph that is not shaded in, represents the illusive attempt to portray a competitor's product as immediately dropping to 90% of its rated value and then remaining there for the first 10 years at which time it abruptly falls again to 80% of its rated value and once again remains there for an additional 15 years. Contrary, the shaded part of the graph is an attempt in an illusion that their product has a gradual descent and provides additional warranty value. As explained earlier, modules do not abruptly lose production value. They all **gradually** decline. This visual scam is a marketing ploy that many module companies have adopted in the past 3-4 years. The reason is simple. There are very few differences between all of the module manufacturing methods and finished products. When "their" finished product is nearly identical to all the competitors' product, companies must get very creative in their marketing strategies. They cannot simply build bigger modules and market theirs as "the biggest" for several reasons. The main reason is that solar modules are bought and sold **by the watt**, not by the each. Secondly, these things are installed by hand not by machine, so there are reasonable limits to their physical size.

Now let's move on to the inverters. We have already spent considerable time in previous chapters on the subject of inverter warranties, however, I would like to elaborate a bit. The most commonly used type of inverter in small-to-medium size installations are "string" inverters. You will recall that a string inverter manages power input from one or more groups (strings) of modules. Typical strings of modules will consist of anywhere between 8 and 16 modules each. So figuratively speaking, a string inverter that has a total array of 28 modules attached to it, will likely have two parallel strings of modules consisting of 14 each. As described earlier, the widely accepted warranty period for these types of inverters is 10 years **from the manufacturer.** As we have discussed, some who provide functioning systems to their clients profess a "power production" guarantee for much longer, however, the actual manufacturer typical warranty is 10 years.

Herein we find a very sneaky potential. I cannot accurately claim that the leasing folks have this intent, but it is possible, so I will reveal the concept. If the language in a lease contract professes a **"power production"** guarantee, it is possible they will be able to legally show their claim as accurate even if the inverter fails during the term of a lease contract. Let's examine what it means to **"produce power"**. As I explained previously, the modules are the "engine" of a functioning solar system. It is precisely the modules that **produce** the solar power. Also as we have learned, the modules will typically come with a 25-year warranty. This is a manufacturer provided warranty and not a product of the lease responsibility. We have also learned that the occurrence in which a module goes bad is very rare. Now let's look at the precise function of the inverter(s). An inverter **does not produce power,** it alters it. Can you see where this is going yet? I'll continue.

If the language in any given contract simply states "guaranteed power production", it is conceivable that this will be accurate **even if the inverter fails.** The inverter **only** receives incoming D.C. power from the modules and alters (inverts) it to A.C. power in order to accommodate the loads and/or grid. It will be very easy for a technician to walk up to an inverter that is non-operational during sunlight hours and by using a basic voltage tester show that the modules are indeed still **"producing power"** even though it is not making its way to the A.C. side of the arrangement. This use of language is extremely important to anyone engaging a leased system. Again, I must be clear that I am not suggesting this will be the case in any or all of the leased relationships; however, it is definitely possible. If a leasing contract does not clearly identify a guaranteed power production **all the way through to the A.C. electrical panel,** it is very suspicious in my opinion.

Also, I have briefly mentioned "microinverters" in past chapters. Typically, this is a small inverter that is assigned to a single solar module. This unit will be mounted directly under its assigned module and basically plugs directly into it. Groups of these are then attached to a common master wire (trunk line) and their grouping of power is sent to the facilities A.C. power location. Currently the solar market is beginning to see what is referred to as "A.C. modules". This actually represents an oxymoron in-and-of itself, simply because solar modules initially produce D.C. (direct current) power. However, this newly adopted method of providing solar modules that have a "built-in" microinverter attached to them is now referred to as an "A.C. module". By themselves, a typical warranty on a microinverter is now 25 years. Upon their introduction and during the first few years of their usage, microinverters boasted a 20 warranty. With the typical module warranty at 25 years, the microinverter folks were very motivated to also establish a 25 year warranty so a window of opportunity to merge the two in the factory would be open. This has been achieved, so we now have a product available known as "A.C. modules".

Even though my opinions are pessimistic in nature toward microinverters, I must be very open and honest with my feelings and thoughts about their **current** quality and longevity likelihood. Due to my personal experiences with microinverters, I would not yet use the A.C. module. In 5-10 more years, maybe, but not now. These types of inverters do not have a history of long-term reliability yet. The concept is very good, however, the technology is still "working out the bugs" in my opinion. For me, a minimum of 10 years **with reliable performance** in continuous "real world" conditions is a must.

If you are one of the many people who have a personal priority of having the "latest and greatest"...I can understand and appreciate that. You are part of the group within the public that provide the "testing grounds" so-to-speak. At my stage of the game however, I require products that will protect my long and slowly earned reputation. I do not want to be in my sixties and have my phone constantly ringing, with clients complaining about a product I sold them in the past. We all must choose for ourselves based on our personal priorities. Much like people, products also must **earn** their own reputations. It is in how each of us defines an "earned reputation" that will determine when we each align ourselves with any given product or person for that matter.

3. Are American made modules better or does it matter?

To answer this, we must divide it into two parts, because there really are two different questions here. First, "Are American made modules better?" In general terms there are usually some aspects that are better and some that are not. Second, "Does it matter?" is absolutely a decision based on personal priorities. What matters to one person may not to another. Let's elaborate on both of these issues. It has been my experience, so far, that the differences in American made are found in the structural aspects of any given module. Electronically speaking, I find no real differences in output or production. The American modules tend to be thicker and heavier in the frame material and/or the tempered glass sheet that covers the entire module. If you are in a state that encounters severe weather, this may be an asset. I have found that in the category of power output, you can basically close your eyes and pick one. Again, I will remind us that solar modules are bought and sold based on the wattage rating, not by the unit. Regardless of their physical dimensions, all modules with comparable wattage ratings will produce extremely similar amounts of power without any discrepancies toward where they are assembled.

When focusing on the output values of solar modules, I have not found one to be better than another due to the country of manufacturing origin. The truth is that modules are predominately assembled in the Asian countries. This has nothing to do with quality and everything to do with costs. Simply put, they can build them with less cost than we can. Consider this:

It currently costs less to ship the raw materials to China (for example), assemble the modules and then ship the finished product, via containers on gigantic ocean going vessels to the U.S., than it does to build them in our backyard. **The fact is that the Asian workforce costs considerably less than the American work force.** As with nearly everything industrial, money is the determining factor.

So, are American made modules better? That depends on your priority. In the structural aspect, they probably are. In the power production aspect, I truly do not believe so. The second part of our question was, "Does it matter?" **I do not ever answer this for my clients.** I have installed a lot of both American and Asian made modules. There is so much that goes into this decision, it can only come from within. Do not allow yourself to be manipulated into the attempts by those who try and decide for you. If this is the case, I believe it is for their own personal gain. Any salesperson that tells you **what matters to you** is moving you toward the product that **they** want to sell you. For my clients, if they have a priority that dictates American made and are willing to pay the mild cost differences, I am designing and then installing a solar system on their property that includes American made modules. I only provide the option, **they decide.** As we move through 2014, it is reasonable to believe that the cost of Asian made modules will show increases in the near future. If so, an increased demand for American made modules could be realized. Depending on the levels of supply and demand for American modules, these too may reveal cost increases. Only time will tell.

4. Is there any maintenance that I will need to do?

There is very little that **needs** to be done to ensure the functionality of a typical solar system providing there are no actual breakdowns with the equipment. However, to ensure the maximum potential for power production, you may **want** to wash the modules periodically. Although this is not really required, it is a good idea as long as you can access the modules safely. I do not encourage the average homeowner to frequent a 2-story roof location to wash their modules. Common sense must be considered. If your system is on a low ground frame with easy access and you can rinse off the dust as it becomes heavy on the surface of the modules, you will indeed increase your production. So how much increase will you realize? That depends on how dirty they are to begin with, the amount of available sunlight hours during the current time of year and the total size of your array.

By the way, **do not** hit the modules with cold water in the middle of a hot day. Treat them much like the windshield of your car. Early or late in the day after the direct, hot sunshine is no longer beating straight down on them. If you are extreme in your tasks and use cleaners, be sure they are **non-abrasive** and **non-corrosive.** A mild eco-friendly liquid dish soap in a bucket of warm water with a very soft brush will work well. Do not think that you **must** wash your modules, it is just something that can help the production values somewhat. I will tell you that of the people I know who do wash their modules, the vast majority simply rinse them off. Most people do not wash them at all, especially if the array is on a rooftop.

A related question I usually get is, "How much will my production increase if I keep them clean?" As mentioned earlier, this will depend on several factors. Here is a real experiment that I did several years ago. My experiment provided a good idea of a percentage value in an agricultural setting. We had installed a 10kW (10,000 watt) system on a small farm location. We put 5,000 watts on a metal roof and the remaining 5,000 watts on a ground frame just in front of the same building. The roof mount array and the ground array each had their own string inverters. In essence, we had two independent systems attached to the same grid location.

We returned to this location one summer morning and found these modules were very dusty. The sun was up in the mid-morning sky but was not directly overhead yet. The dust was heavy enough to write your name in it, however, there were no "heavy duty" issues such as bird droppings etc. I had one guy watch the "read outs" on the display screen of the inverters and another guy simply use a hose and rinse off the dust on the ground array starting at one end and proceeding to the other end. Immediately after completing the rinsing we saw a gradual increase in production that equated to approximately 10%. Some of this increase was no doubt caused by the cooling effect the water had on the modules. It was probably in the neighborhood of 75–80° F as we conducted this test. However, the majority of the production increase was due to the removal of the dust from the module surfaces. In my estimation, there was approximately a 2% increase due to the cooling effect and an 8% increase due to cleaning. So cleaning obviously helped in a very dirty location such as a farm. But before you decide you are going to clean your array every day, be sure you consider all the ingredients. How much water are you consuming to do this? Are you paying someone such as an employee to perform this task? Is your array location safe and easy to access? Be sure to balance all of your priorities when it comes to cleaning your modules.

As far as any other maintenance concerns, there is really

only one other small one that should be considered a couple of times per year in normal conditions. String inverters have an internal cooling fan that circulates air throughout the inverter. The "intake" portion of these fans will have a mesh screen to filter out debris. This screen should be kept free of heavy debris that can severely restrict incoming air. **Do not** open the inverter housing in search of this screen. It will be easily accessible from the outside. Consult the owner's manual for the locations of these screens.

Before I close out this section, there is one more area that is usually not used, but on occasion can be a sales promotion – "Maintenance Contracts". As we have just learned, the maintenance on a typical, modest solar array is mostly voluntary and has a very limited effect on its performance. Do not be convinced by a salesperson that says, "To keep your investment in tip-top shape for many years, we need to take care of it." The next thing you know you have signed an expensive agreement that will never pay for itself. Clean modules will not last any longer than dirty ones. The module warranties do not state that the modules must remain clean. In nearly every case, the dollar value of the modest increase in production will not come close to paying for that illusive maintenance agreement. A typical, functioning, grid interactive solar system without batteries or a tracker should be very close to maintenance free.

5. *What if the grid power goes out? Will I have power still? Do I have to do anything to the solar when the power comes back on?*

As mentioned earlier, the most common type of solar usage is a grid interactive system that has a purpose of offsetting the kWh's consumed. With this type of system, the solar power production will cease when the associated grid source is absent. The inverter(s) have a basic requirement for them to function. Both voltages need to be present simultaneously. You will recall that voltage represents electrical pressure. The voltage coming from the solar modules in one direction, along with the voltage coming from the grid in the other direction. If either of these voltages are absent the inverter will not function. This actually takes place every night. With the sunlight departing in the evening, the inverter(s) shut down. If the grid were to depart, again the inverter(s) shut down.

A brief explanation that I frequently use is with a typical playground teeter-totter. The inverter represents the center balancing point. If either side is weightless (without voltage), there is an out-of-balance present. The inverter must have balance which is represented by available voltage on both sides.

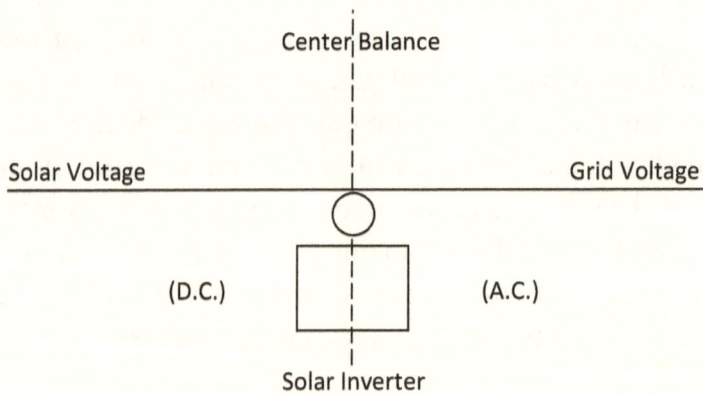

This also becomes an extremely important safety factor. If the grid were to go down during the day, with all the solar arrays in the area making their power, and the inverter(s) allowed the solar power to pass through, the otherwise down grid (utility) would become energized.

It is a common assumption by many people that with their

own solar power generation system onsite, they will still have power during grid outages. As we have now learned, this is not the case. So with this understanding, the next question is, "Do I need to do anything with the solar when the grid returns?" Usually not. The inverter(s) constantly "search" for both forms of voltage. As shown above they need both voltages to allow the function of power to flow. Just as with every early morning that brings the return of sunlight, so does the return of grid voltage have the same effect on the inverter. If it is daytime and the sunlight is sufficient but the utility (grid) voltage is absent, the inverter is "idle" while it searches for the balance in voltage. Upon the return of grid voltage, the inverter will engage itself without any assistance from you in nearly every case. However, there can be those rare situations in which the inverter did not restart itself automatically.

It is always a good idea to check and make sure all is good. If your system is not functioning within 10-15 minutes of the return of utility power and there is sufficient sunlight, locate the inverter disconnect switch (typically a round quarter-turn dial) and turn it off. Wait 15 minutes or so and turn it back on. On occasion, this can reset the inverters recognition of what it is "seeing" from the available power sources. If this does not work, you likely have a bad internal fuse. Call your installer or a qualified individual to check it out. **At no time** should an unqualified person remove the covers from the inverter. The D.C. voltage from the solar array is typically between 300-500 volts! This should not be messed with by just anyone.

6. *Is there a way to have my own power still on when the utility grid goes down?*

Yes. This is referred to as a "back-up" system. Depending on your geographical area, finding qualified designers and installers may be a real challenge. This is only due to the lack of demand. If this type of system were commonplace, many would become involved for financial reasons. However, in most populated areas in which solar power is desired, few realize grid outages that are either frequent enough or long enough to justify the moderately higher costs associated with having a "back-up" power source(s) on standby.

Let me take a moment to explain how a grid-tied solar system can also function when the utility grid is down. Previously we learned that a typical inverter needs both solar (D.C.) voltage and grid (A.C.) voltage to function. This is true for the reasons we already discussed. But now let's consider how and why a solar system **can** work even without the grid voltage available. Beyond all the obvious and necessary safety aspects as revealed earlier, there are also physical aspects between the nature of the provided power (grid and/or solar) and the consumed power (loads).

For your understanding, a "load", in electrical terms, is anything that uses electricity. A typical load such as lights, your refrigerator, your hair dryer or anything else that operates by "plugging it in" in North America uses A.C. (alternating current). This type of power is based on a relatively constant and even flow of power. In other words, your refrigerator wants to "see" a power source that fluctuates very little. The standards by which electrical components are built to withstand, as far as power fluctuations are concerned, is +/- 10%. So if your refrigerator is designed to operate on 120 volts A.C. (and most are) it can go unharmed in a situation that may see the voltage drop to 108 volts or increase to 132 volts, which equates to -10% and +10% respectively.

Now imagine that all you have for a power source is your typical solar system. Without a component of **storage,** your system is completely at the mercy of the available sunlight. What this means is that the product of continuous and steady power flow is unlikely during certain conditions and impossible during others. A solar system is directly and very quickly affected by the brightness and angle of the sun. The same system may be producing 5000 watts at any given moment, only to have a thick cloud float in front of the sun, and suddenly the wattage may fall to half of that.

Solar productivity changes very routinely in certain weather conditions, time of day and even seasonally (time of year). So with the understanding that your loads (refrigerator, lights, etc.) require a somewhat constant and stable flow of wattage (power), you can realize that a typical solar system alone will not provide that. This is where a storage component comes in. Batteries are nothing more than a storage container for power. Much like a water tank stores water, so do batteries store power. Whenever you have a situation in which there is a need for stable and steady power output, but the input (supply) is unstable and routinely changing, you need to insert a "buffer" between them. Consider this analogy with the sketch below.

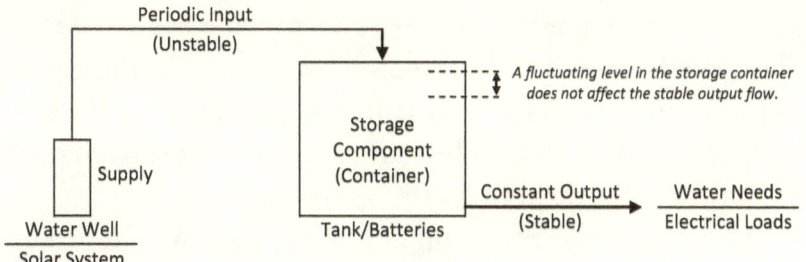

By cross-referencing water and electrical components we can easily understand the importance of a buffer or storage component. The tank or batteries in this case, provide a constant and steady output flow by allowing a fluctuation within the levels of stored water or power in the container. The supply source (well or solar) only needs to operate frequently and long enough as to maintain some available product (water or power) in the container. By introducing batteries in our complete solar system, we have now provided for the storage of power onsite in the event the utility grid goes down.

I have given you the basic description of why batteries are necessary in a typical "back-up" system. I must also make clear that there is **much more** that goes into a quality solar system with back-up power capabilities. This becomes a very involved set of components, so finding someone who actually understands how it all works **together** is not very common. If a back-up system, including batteries, is something you are seriously contemplating, I strongly encourage you to **delay purchasing or installing any portion of your solar system** until you have a very clear understanding of the final arrangement of all the components. **Do not** purchase and install a typical system from someone who tells you that "their company doesn't do back-up systems, but you can have someone else add that later". It does not work that way. Likewise, you will not find a large "cookie cutter" company that functions on volume, with the understanding or desire to provide such a system. The overall demand for back-up systems is very low in general and nearly non-existent in urban settings, therefore the large companies do not play in this game. There is not enough profit or frequency for them to do so.

Now let's spend a few minutes on a type of system that can be much simpler and more common in rural settings. In essence this is a typical solar system that is grid interactive, does not include batteries for power storage, but does have a back-up component. In this situation a generator is used. By introducing a generator, the need for a storage component is removed due to the continuous and steady operation of the generator. Providing the generator is in good mechanical condition and has an ample fuel supply, it can function continuously regardless of weather conditions or seasons of the year etc.

There are limitations of power output that are based on the individual size of the output capabilities in each unit. It becomes very unlikely a generator would be used in urban settings simply because of the noise factor and fuel storage issues. In this type of application whereas there are no batteries acting as a storage vessel, the solar system is identical to our standard grid-tied situation. All the same parameters and functions apply. The generator is attached to a load panel that is segregated from the main utility supply panel by means of a "transfer switch". This can be a manual or automatic switch. This switch has a single purpose only. It insures that the utility source and the generators power do not ever comingle simultaneously.

It can only be one or the other when it comes to the availability of grid power **or** a generators power providing the supply to the designated loads. So in the event of a grid power outage, the typical solar inverter shuts down thus rendering the solar system idle, the transfer switch is moved, either manually or automatically to the "generator" position, which in turn disengages the utility source, and the generator is started. When the grid power is restored, the generator is turned off, the transfer switch is moved back to the "grid" position and if enough sunlight is available, the solar inverter restarts. I must also insist here, that only someone who is qualified and **understands** this type of system perform the installation. If installed incorrectly, the generator and the solar inverter could conflict thus causing severe damage.

Generally speaking, a back-up system becomes a luxury in many cases due to the infrequency and/or short lengths of time the utility grid is down. However, if your situation dictates, a back-up system can be a great addition. Do your homework. Look at all the options for **your** situation based on your location, power needs, etc. But above all else, find a qualified person or company that really understands the complexities of how the grid, solar power and the various back-up methods coexist.

I should also mention that for larger needs, any combination of solar power, multiple back-up methods and the grid can be combined. I have done many systems that incorporated the utility grid, a solar system with battery storage and a generator. I have even done systems that had all of the above components and also included small wind turbines. Likewise, I have done many water wells that involved solar pumps that have the capability to operate on grid power, generator power or solar power alone. With the current availability of components and a good understanding of how they all work, the options are very good these days for your power choices.

7. Can I install a solar system that will allow me to detach from the grid permanently?

Yes, but... I have found that this is becoming an increasingly popular desire. If you are attached to a typical utility grid as the vast majority of us are, you are directly involved with one of the last true monopoly's in the private sector in this country. If you really stop and consider all of the areas in your life in which you have choices, you will realize that your electrical power supply is not one of them. In fact, you will probably have a hard time coming up with anything else that represents such an entrenched monopoly.

The point is, that in our current times, choices are everywhere except our power source. You only have one set of wires passing by your property. It is basically a "take it or leave it" situation. The psychology of a human being will show a resistance to confinement. In other words, we search for freedom. The lack of choices directly correlates to the lack of freedom. With this awareness, the availability of establishing your own personal power supply 24/7 is becoming an increasingly popular point of interest.

I must address this issue from a realistic position. There are really two main forces that drive a desire such as power independence. The first is the freedom aspect as we just described and the second is an availability and/or financial aspect. I will tell you that so far, with our current utility pricing structures, the financial aspect is very hard to justify providing the utility power supply is already located on your property and in close proximity to your desired location of your loads. To put this in simple terms, if you are building a house close to the utility power lines, you will pay less overall through the years by purchasing utility power than by purchasing and maintaining a self-sufficient off-grid system. So obviously, if you already have grid power connected, it will not be financially lucrative for you to disconnect and install an off-grid system that will perform to the same capacity as the grid now does.

In urban settings this is not really a valuable consideration for many reasons. However, in rural settings there are circumstances that can suggest an off-grid system is financially wise. For instance, if you are building a house that is a long distance away from the nearest utility power supply, the cost to bring the utility power to you may be substantial. From an availability standpoint, if the grid in your area suffers very long outages due to weather etc., having a more reliable supply may be worth the investment. Typically speaking though, this situation would suggest a back-up system and not an isolated off-grid system.

Finally, we should acknowledge those who simply prefer self-sufficiency. If this is your priority **and** your location is accommodating **and** money is not an issue, then by all means you can create your own self-sufficient and completely off-grid power system. This will not be a wise endeavor by just doing research and/or training on the internet. The **value in experience** with such scenarios is an absolute priority in my opinion. Please do not tackle this type of project without someone who has adequate experience in this arena and who involves themselves due to desire not just money. Attitude is vital in the pursuit of off-grid power systems.

8. Are there any "incentives" to install solar?

When I am asked this question, it is always delivered as a financial inquiry. Although there are obvious "green" incentives, I am not qualified to reveal any quantities. I cannot personally tell you how much carbon is displaced from the environment with the implementation of any given solar system. This is not because I do not believe this is an important aspect, but because this is not why most people acquire a solar system. As I said earlier in this book, "If solar does not provide a reasonable return-on-investment, this industry would cease in general." The "green" aspect is a very worthwhile ingredient for sure, but that is not why 9 out of 10 people get a solar system. The reality is simply that it has to be a wise investment financially. So with this reality, I focus on the "choice aspect" and the "financial aspect" with all of my clients.

Now let's consider the availability of incentives as they relate to monetary value in the use of solar products. Overall, throughout the U.S., there is currently a 30% Federal Income Tax credit available toward the implementation of any approved alternative energy system. This offers a 30% credit based on the total cost of the installed system. **This credit follows the ownership of the equipment.** Even if the equipment is installed on property that you legally own but the solar equipment is owned by others, it is them not you that has access to this tax credit. You may recall, we discussed this in length in a previous chapter. Please understand this process prior to any final decisions pertaining to a method of acquisition.

Next, there could be any number of local rebate programs or cash incentives available. Typically these types of programs are set up as an initial "jump start" to promote the usage of alternative energy products in a given geographical area. They may be confined to individual utility districts or encompass an entire state. You will need to do your own local research to determine if such programs exist in your area. If grants are your thing, you will likely find state and/or federal grant opportunities for certain applications. Typically these will pertain to commercial and/or agricultural usages. It is not the intent of government grants to help supply the individual homeowner application.

While on the subject of commercial and/or agricultural solar usage, we have previously mentioned the ability to "depreciate" the system costs after the 30% Federal Tax Credit is deducted for systems applied to businesses. This basically allows for the remaining costs of a fully installed solar system, minus the 30% tax credit, to be considered an expense toward the individual business that owns the equipment. A good place to start your research to determine if this applies to you, is by looking up the process referred to as "M.A.C.R.S." This stands for: "Modified Accelerated Cost Recovery System". In addition, it would seem reasonable to expect most up-to-date and well-qualified tax professionals to be very aware of the current tax laws in conjunction with the **ownership** of solar products that are installed as a **functioning system.** This last statement is very important! **The tax credit and/or deprecation is only applied to the owner of the equipment once installed and functioning.** A warehouse storing these products does not qualify. Be sure your tax advisor (if you have such) is up to speed on the current tax laws.

Currently, the above-mentioned financial incentives are extremely important to the widespread usage of solar products in the private sector. Should the 30% Federal Tax Credit be drastically reduced or eliminated altogether, the growth of the solar industry would be severely affected. As we have discussed throughout this book thus far, the solar industry has more than its share of coming internal issues. The continuation of a substantial tax credit is absolutely vital to the future of this industry in the general population.

9. What if I need to replace my roofing in a few years after I install solar on it?

This will greatly depend on how you obtained your solar system. If you own it yourself, your experience will consist of paying a qualified person or company to remove the components on the roof and then reinstall them following the roofing replacement. This will pose a moderate expense and present a need to store the equipment during the roofing change-out.

This is by far the "best case" scenario. If you are involved with a lease contract during which time you discover a need to replace your roofing material that is in conjunction with the solar equipment, your experience will be much more difficult, if not downright frustrating! If you are contemplating entering into a solar lease contract, (and I haven't talked you out of it yet), **be absolutely as sure as you can that your roofing will out-live your lease contract.**

Next, do not let a solar salesperson be the one to tell you the remaining life expectancy of your roofing material. Have someone who is actually qualified to install roofing, and **has ample experience in doing so,** be your advisor. 15 or 20 year leasing contracts that are used to place "built-in", permanent solar equipment on a roof that has 10 years of life expectancy left in it, will become a very big problem in the future. Becoming entangled in a situation of having a leaking roof while you are struggling with getting the solar equipment removed by a company that may or may not still exist, can be extremely damaging. Think ahead before you succumb to that very well trained salesperson.

Also, there is really no such thing as a "forever" roof. If you have any type of composition or tar based materials, yours is the most likely to need replacing sometime in the future. Even though tile roofing is routinely referred to as "lifetime", I have seen those occasions where the tar paper breaks down under the tile and leaks develop. The tile may be "lifetime", but the water barrier underlayment is not. In my opinion, the closest type of roofing material that is commonly used and that represents the longest lasting without leaks when properly installed would be most forms of metal. Certain localized climate conditions will play a big part in the most accepted and valuable type of roofing.

The overall point is to be aware of your roofs condition prior to placing a long-term "permanent" product on it. If you own this product, you can control its removal and reinstallation. If someone else owns the product on your roof, you do not have total control over what takes place on **your** roof.

10. Can I add to my solar system later if I start out with a small one initially?

Again, depending on how you initially obtained your system will the ease in which you can add later be determined. Also, once again, if you have leased your system, this may be extremely difficult if not simply impermissible completely. As I have repeatedly shown, many restrictions accompany a typical solar lease. However, on the "bright side" it is actually quite simple providing there are not space or electrical limitations.

Solar is configured in "groupings" physically speaking. A group (array) of modules is assigned to a single string inverter or a group of modules/micro inverters are assigned to a common master wire (trunk line). These groupings can be compiled at a common location and all connected to the same utility grid service on site. So you may start out with a string inverter that has a couple dozen modules attached to it and then later add a second inverter with its own modules also being added. This can be repeated until the space is depleted or the maximum capacity of the existing main utility service is matched.

Unlike our inspector in a previous chapter who did not understand this concept, a solar generating power system can be as large, in amperage capacity, as is the associated utility service at this same location. Proving the arrangement and sizes of all the main components are connected together in a proper sequence and the correct connection methods are used (as ours were) the allowable solar system size can equal the utility grid service size in ampacity ratings. With this understanding, we know our limitations from the beginning. In a previous example we used a common solar system size of 5,000 watts for a home. In America, the typical residence will have an incoming grid service that is based on 240 volts A.C. The amperage rating of this incoming utility service is typically between 100 amps and 200 amps, with the occasional 400 amp service on larger homes. Remember this basic equation that is the foundation of how power is generated and consumed:

$$\text{Volts} \times \text{Amps} = \text{Watts}$$
$$\text{Watts} \div \text{Amps} = \text{Volts}$$
$$\text{Watts} \div \text{Volts} = \text{Amps}$$

These are all synonymous. If you know any two of these three products, you can always identify the missing third product by using one of these equations. So now back to our example. If a solar system has a maximum potential of producing 5000 watts and we know it is attached to a grid that occupies 240 volts A.C., then: 5000 watts ÷ 240 volts = 20.8 amps. Thus, this solar inverter would likely be attached via a protective fuse or O.C.P.D. (over current protection device) rated at 25 amps. As we can easily determine, this rating is far less than any of the typical main service ratings found on most homes.

With this knowledge and by using the proper attachment methods, even a home with a small 100 amp main service could realize a much larger solar application than our example of a 5,000 watt system. As we can see, adding to a system in the future is very doable as long as the needed space is available and the proper grid attachment method is used.

With the establishment of this option, let's look at the "how's" and "why's" of exercising an enlargement. If you believe your electrical consumption is going to moderately increase within a 3-5 year timeframe, you may choose to initially install a larger inverter than is currently necessary. With a plan of future growth in place, a large inverter can begin with fewer modules and take on additional modules later. I do not suggest this type of maneuver if your expected time of increase is beyond 5 years in the future. Assuming a lifespan of 10 years on the average inverter, I would suggest starting with an adequately sized inverter now and simply adding another inverter at which time you decide to increase the overall size of your system.

Another important consideration is within the expected availability of modules. Although inverters do not care about brands of modules, the voltage and wattage of common modules on a single inverter can be crucial in preserving a maximum potential of output. For example, if you start with a string of modules that are rated at 250 watts each with an expected voltage output of 30 volts each, the most important factor in the future addition of more modules will be the 30 volt expected output of the additional modules. The inverter will recognize the lowest available voltage in the modules and pull all of them to that voltage in a typical array with our most common types of inverters used today. So the least amount of discrepancy between the voltage outputs of the old and new modules the better.

Although it is somewhat important, the discrepancy in module wattages is not as crucial. If a wattage discrepancy of 10 watts per module exists between old and new modules, very little effect will be realized providing the voltage outputs of the modules are relatively close. So because of the continuously changing module sizes, it is risky to plan on adding more modules to an existing inverter too many years out into the future. It is much safer to go with a small inverter and a group of modules now, then do it again when the time comes. In this way you have not comingled old and new components.

We have now discussed, in some detail, the top ten questions I routinely get from potential clients. There is one other topic of conversation that comes up very often these days, that is centered on the overwhelming confusion in the public's awareness concerning whether to lease or purchase. I feel I have spent adequate time explaining my position on this topic along with my reasons. At this point, I believe any further discussion on my part would simply become redundant.

I will however, share a somewhat new and slowly increasing trend. When I recorded my radio commercial in 2010, nobody I ever heard spoke negatively about the solar leases, except myself and Andrew and possibly those people who were against any type of non-ownership financing. But now, very gradually, some of you are finally starting to get it. Within the past year or so, it has become no surprise when I hear a potential client tell me that they do not like the idea of what the solar lease represents. Finally, people are beginning to say such things to me before I have to say anything. I personally believe that the concept and practice of the solar leasing industry, as we know it today, has reached its peak. As people become more aware of the looming issues contained within these agreements and simultaneously the lending institutions continue to increase their lending practices to a greater number of people pursing solar, I truly believe the solar leasing game is going to begin its inevitable descent. I only hope it doesn't take an entire industry down with it, like we all experienced in the mortgage industry few short years ago. As with everything, time will tell.

CLOSING COMMENTS

As I consider any final thoughts and feelings that would be important to share within this book, it occurs to me that much of the "tone" I have presented thus far appears troublesome and maybe even harsh on occasion. If this is how you have received my delivery, it is important for me to clarify my position on solar energy, the products, and its usage.

The fact is that I believe so much in the overall benefits of what solar does for **people**, not to mention the environment, that it is within my passion for its use that you will find my disappointments. Our technologies have finally given us a product that's very reliable and beneficial. I cannot remember all of my clients whom I've left with an installed system that have remained very happy after two years, three years, and in fact, for as many years as I have had solar clients. I run into these people routinely at the grocery store, gas station, etc. It really has a tremendous effect on me personally to hear from a past client as they express their total satisfaction with something I helped them acquire.

For all of you who are reading this, and are actually in the profession of selling/installing solar, I wish to ask you a very serious question. **How do you look at your clients?** Many of you, no, actually I'll bet **most** of you, view your next client as **your** next source of money. The majority of you will deny this initially, but I would suggest that you notice your emotional state as you read my question. If your first priority is your pay-check, then you have simply jumped on the proverbial band-wagon. You are "doing solar" because it has become popular and you can make money in it. If this is you, I will boldly tell you that you are a **follower** not a leader. Sadly, you are among the majority of the newly formed army that is now involved in this industry. Every hybrid car, complete with its full body wrap proclaiming a solar company called "Sun..." or "Solar...", has a salesperson running to their next appointment to tell that potential client that all they need to do is, "Sign here, no money down, it's the right thing to do and we'll be back in six months to install. And by the way, your new solar system will work for 20 years because we say it will."

Next, the box truck also complete with a full body wrap showing off its picture of a big sun and a logo that will "hook you" into believing this is the thing to do, will show up (six months later). Piling out of this truck will be a workforce of guys eager to earn **their next paycheck.** Two years ago they were mowing lawns, framing walls, pouring concrete, nailing on roofing, etc. It's hard to blame them; they have found a full-time job that pays decent. Their boss keeps telling them how much work is lined up, so they are motivated to produce. Meanwhile, back at the office, the salespeople must continue to make their quota of sales calls; the machine needs to be fed. People are out "canvassing" the neighborhoods, hanging fliers on doors, ringing doorbells, etc. All of this is making the in-vestors that provide the access to this equipment, very wealthy. The salespeople and workforce have a steady income as long as this "bubble" is intact, and the current popular frenzy that everybody is talking about (solar) gains even more momentum.

The psychology of a "herd" creature such as the human being makes it somewhat easy for salespeople to invite you to be a part of, "what everybody is now doing". Everyone is, "going solar, so don't be left out". Please understand I am extremely happy that this technology provides access for **a choice** where one did not exist before with nearly everyone who consumes grid power. My overall purpose with this book is to make known the threats that I believe will damage the public's opinion of this very positive technology. **This book is quite simply a warning.** When this "bubble" finally bursts, it is my personal priority to make as many people aware as I can reach, that it had **nothing to do with the benefits of the products, but everything to do with the priorities of the people who dominated this industry's methods of acquisition.** It is a simple matter of David and Goliath so-to-speak. The very few of us who do not participate in the lease arrangements, represent a small minority of the total number of solar acquisitions. The solar lease has become the image of the solar industry. This way of obtaining solar is so large, that many within the public do not even consider a different path. They have come to a pre-conceived conclusion that their only choice is which company to use. Excellent marketing strategies and perfect timing have created our current industry and how it is perceived by the general population.

For those of you who do wish to obtain these products for your own usage and are not interested in renting them for 15 or 20 years, I will tell you to pursue this endeavor by looking for a supplier/installer who has a history in your local area and preferably actually lives there. If you live in a small town or a rural setting, you will likely need to do business with a non-resident. This does not pose a problem as long as this company can produce a **long list** of referrals that have purchased systems from them. **Learn who the owner(s) are.** Dealing with a salesperson is fine, but is there access to those whose reputations are on the line? Even if you do not deal with them directly, absolutely know who they are and what their history represents. It is very easy for an abstract investor/owner to "evaporate" if things go bad. A **visible, well-known owner** will be much more interested in their personal reputation than will an invisible ownership body.

Next, many of you are wondering if **now** is the right time to buy solar. Are costs going to reduce and/or technologies greatly improve? These two questions cause a lot of you to ask, "When is the time right?" Although I cannot and will not speak for what is right for any of you specifically; I will share the recent history and my opinions of what the near future holds for the "cost and technology" questions.

We will begin with 2007, because that is when solar, photo-voltaic, was attempting to establish itself as a valuable product to the private sector. As with nearly every new industry, costs start out high and eventually reduce as the demand triggers a much larger supply. In new or even small demand industries, the manufacturing mechanism is running in first gear. Due to low demand of the product, it is manufactured in small quantities. Also, there are fewer companies participating so the competition is much less. All of this typically reveals high costs to the consumer. Such was the case in 2007, 2008, and even 2009.

I will say that for those of you who are purchasing your solar systems now, or even in the past year or so, the big leasing companies have done you a big favor. Because of the overall demand that has materialized in the past 3-4 years, the manufacturing sector has ramped up to high gear. Also, hundreds of companies have joined in. This means big competition and a huge availability of product. With this, module costs have plummeted. Modules that cost between $3.50 per watt and $4.00 per watt in 2007 now cost $1.00 per watt in some cases.

Module costs are typically 300-400% lower than they were in 2007 as compared to now in 2014.

Now I must warn you procrastinators. We are all done with significant cost decreases in solar modules. In fact, we have been stable in module costs for the past year. I would look for the modest increases to begin anytime and slowly creep up as we traverse 2015. Here is why I believe this will be the case. The U.S. government is involving a tariff on Chinese modules. This will be passed on to the consumer. Also, of the hundreds of manufacturers and brands of modules, many are beginning to go away. Mergers are taking place, less established companies closing their doors, etc. The large producers have driven costs so low, that the small producers can't operate and compete. In essence, the "heavy hitters" are eliminating their competition. Another factor is that the political climate in China has a lot to do with who is in business and who is not in their country. As these ingredients take hold and cause a shift in the supply and demand equation, costs will slowly rise. Add to this, all of the looming issues that I have suggested throughout this book, that will likely start having an effect on the public's opinion of solar in general in the coming few years, and a lower demand is very probable.

All of this is based on one assumption on my part. I am assuming that the state and federal governments do not come up with some type of an all inclusive, very enticing incentive program. Currently we do have the 30% Federal Tax Credit that, in my opinion, is the only reason the solar industry has remained and grown. Without this tax credit, the leases do not exist and the return on investment timeframe for purchasers is much longer. Note: As of now, the 30% tax credit is scheduled to end on December 31, 2016. So if the incentive structure were to become much better than 30%, we could in fact see continued growth and somewhat stable module costs despite the troubles that await the leasing relationships.

If you have decided to purchase a solar system, but are waiting for costs to hit bottom, wait no longer. So now it will depend on your priorities. If you really want to obtain solar, do it soon. If you are "lukewarm" in your attitude toward your involvement, then waiting for a better incentive program from the next administration in 2016 (and beyond) may or may not pay off. If you are inclined to wait for a better deal, be sure you factor in the continued utility costs you are paying while you wait. I believe it is a safe bet that your utility costs over the next 2+ years will be more than the "better deal" will save you, if it actually materializes. One thing is for sure when it comes to the stability of the solar industry in this country – **it isn't.**

Now let's look at module technologies. Remember our previous discussions concerning the efficiencies of modules? Modules have simply been slowly increasing their power rating size without increasing their physical dimensions. What was a 220 watt module 3-4 years ago is now a 250 watt module. On average, we see a 5-10 watt increase each year in the power ratings of solar modules while remaining the same dimensions. Also, the standard silicon cell module that is built as a single unit in its own frame is by far the most common.

New technologies are no doubt out there some day, but I surely would not wait for a major breakthrough. Even if something drastically different were to hit the market tomorrow, I would strongly suggest a minimum of 5 years before I would use it. We have seen the "thin film" products show up and then basically go nowhere. The "integrated tile" products are only used selectively in certain applications. The "double-sided" module that supposedly gathers light from both sides is not anywhere near the point of widespread, cost effective use. Our current silicon based modules allow placement over any type of roofing materials along with having the rigidity to mount to a skeletal type ground frame. A good rule of thumb is to figure a production value of approximately 1,000 watts of solar power for every 100 square feet of space covered by the modules. This is a rough calculation that is dependent on your location, angle of the sun, exposure, etc. This is also for a stationary array that is not affected by shade.

I believe module technologies will continue at their current modest pace of improvement and eventually reveal modules that can show a power rating of 300-350 watts each in our current physical sizes. It is very important that you remember that solar modules are bought and sold by the watt. Regardless of the size of each module involved, you will pay for your system by the combined total wattage of that system. **Always** compare costs by the **cost per watt** before any rebates or tax incentives. This represents a true and unaltered comparison on the complete package.

Equally important is knowing whether you are looking at the "D.C." or "A.C." wattage rating of a complete system. The D.C. rating is always larger and basically useless. This does not factor in any losses due to conductors, components, etc. To find the D.C. rating of a system you simply multiply the total module quantity by the module rating. Example, 24 total modules and each is 250 watts so 24 x 250 = 6,000 D.C. watts. There is a lot more in the way of calculations that go into the determination of the A.C. wattage size. Typically speaking, any given system will loose 8-13% of its rating capacity due to losses in wiring and components. So this same system containing 24 modules of 250 watts each, that has a D.C. rating of 6,000 watts, will likely reveal an A.C. rating of 5,200-5,500 watts. With all of this now known, it is my opinion that the cost per A.C. watt, prior to any incentives, is the most direct and sure way to compare. Make sure you are comparing equally inclusive installations along with comparable methods.

Let's also take a minute here to talk about financing. In the past year or so, we have seen more and more banks and credit unions come out of hiding. They are now beginning to show signs of life and are actually loaning on solar systems. In my local area, I know of a credit union that has a loan product specifically designed for solar applications and homeowners. Two of my recent clients have used this product of financing and both have given me extremely positive feedback. This is very bad news for the leasing companies and their investors. This represents a legitimate loan structure that is completely based on the client's ownership of the solar products and all the incentives. This provides a real competition based on integrity that will threaten their dominance.

This type of acquisition eliminates all of the potential problems that I have spent a considerable amount of time revealing in this book in conjunction with the lease. The point is that the methods by which more people can obtain these products are increasing. This also represents choices where the portrayal has otherwise been suggesting that none existed. If your only choice is doing nothing or making a bad business decision, do you really have to think about it for very long? Of course, "a bad business decision" is a matter of opinion and perspective. From the perspective of big money people who fund the leasing programs, a huge portion of you have been making great business decisions! Although, when the equipment fails prior to the completion of your contract with them, what will you do? You do not know who they are. You only know their representative and they are not returning your calls. (Sorry, that just slipped out. I've spent more than enough time bashing the lease.)

If your local banks and/or credit unions are still not offering a good loan product for solar systems, it is only a matter of time, providing this industry becomes popular in your part of the world. So far, it seems only the smaller financing institutions are participating. I do not think the mega banks want to be bothered with doing a lot of $20,000-$30,000 loans. They prefer to play with millions I guess.

Well I feel like I've said all that I can say to provide you with the information that few outside of the solar industry have. With this, I will end with a few personal comments. Everything I have shared comes with my truest sincerity. I have not intentionally exaggerated or created one bit of information. Although some of you will have differing opinions on portions of my subject matter, I am committed to my perspectives. If time proves some of my outlooks are incorrect, I will be happy that this industry remained healthier than I anticipated. This book is not about me being right; it's about awareness and exposure. I often say to people, "Give me a load of solar components, **an aware client,** and we have the makings of a very good relationship." I am very content with the niche I have established. My ultimate desire for the solar industry is that it continues...

Despite the opportunistic investors who do not really care about the end user, despite the contractors who aren't really passionate about installing solar but see it as a money source, despite the building inspectors and their peers who are lacking in knowledge and try to cover it up with egos and misconduct, and despite the misunderstandings that so much of the public has about these products and what represents the best way to obtain them. Despite all of this, I just want to see this industry continue in an ethical manner that is founded in integrity. I will admit that I am skeptical of this outcome at this point in time, but then anything is possible.

The final segment to follow sums up the current foundation of this industry. I will close out this first edition of the books called "Solar Integrity" with a list of ingredients we should all be aware of. If enough of you become aware of the potential problems, then just maybe we can all accept the responsibility of change. I believe an entire industry depends on a substantial change to its own status quo if it is to remain healthy in the next decade and for the next generation.

An Industry Born into Dependency

When an entire industry has defined itself through an array of ingredients that have very little history to learn from and are created and controlled by a small few who stand to gain the most, a questionable future is on the horizon. The following list reveals the current structure of the U.S. solar industry.

1. The solar industry in America is a mere 8-10 years old as we know it. We do not have an established history to learn from. During the infantile portion of any widespread industry, the level of integrity that is employed by its pioneers is crucial to the future growth and stability of that industry. Is this industry built on integrity?

2. A very manageable control of the products and/or services associated with a new endeavor is also extremely important. As we have shown, the solar modules are the most expensive and visible component in any fully functional system. Currently the solar industry in this country depends on imported inexpensive modules. This gives us very little manageable control. We are simply a customer not an internal supplier of our own products.

Cost increases, availability issues, governmental tariffs, and even international relationships can all drastically alter the flow of our primary product. Does that represent a manageable control?

3. A stable, long-term, and fair flow of money through any industry is vital. When a "disconnect" is present between the "providers" and "users" of the primary capital that is supporting an industry, it becomes very easy for the providers to wear an invisible disguise. A bank has an actual building that the users of the money walk into, thus the provider is visible. If the provider is only available to you in the form of a contract that is delivered to you by a representative, there is no physical contact or location, thus the provider is invisible. Integrity is now at risk of being absent when the providers are not visible and exposed. A detachment between the "known providers" and "known receivers" removes a "felt" physical responsibility when the "energy" between human beings is exposed. Do all of the people who have signed a long-term lease contract have any physical awareness or place of physical contact to those they are now legally connected to?

4. A new industry that is attempting to establish itself on a widespread scale, in which the public's connection is with an acquisition of a product, must have a high level of public desire to own that product. If, in fact, the public is primarily reacting due to governmental incentives that entice participation, the product is only accepted by the public as long as the incentives are available. Such incentives should only be a factor during the introductory stage of a new product. Once the product is established

within the publics desire to own it, this product should be capable of achieving continued growth and acceptance due to the benefits it provides. If the dependency on a government credit or rebate remains as an absolute necessity after 6-8 years of widespread product availability, this product is not capable of self-sustained growth in a normal market condition. Do any of you really believe the solar industry in the U.S. would remain in tact should the Federal Tax Credit of 30% cease? If an entire industry is dependent on a government incentive for its realistic survival, is this industry on stable ground? Have the few who actually **own** the products convinced the public to rent it long-term?

5. A new industry that brings with it a large monetary investment in which the product becomes a long-term part of the individuals' real estate must insure a high degree of quality in both the product itself and the service personnel who manufacture, distribute, sell, and install the product. With a product that possesses a long life, the amount of "repeat" clients are very limited, therefore new clients are a continual priority.

    Localized reputations play an enormous role in the acquisition of new clients. The provider/installer is the only one in direct contact with the client (end user) and is **very dependent on the entire support structure behind the product.** Should product quality and/or the integrity of any of the entities required to supply the product become suspect, the future **reputation of the provider/installer is at a tremendous risk.** As I have shown throughout this book, the support structure currently involved in the U.S. solar industry is full of inadequate and/or insincere personnel. With the expected functionality of solar products to be 10-25 years, we are nearing a point in time whereas the earlier systems will begin to fail.

When the equipment fails, who does the client (equipment user) first turn to as a means of remedy? The wholesale distributor? The financing entity? The manufacturer? The provider/installer? What if the client **does not legally own** the equipment needing repair? Is this client now completely dependent on the integrity of the entity with whom the open contract is made with?

I have just revealed the five main ingredients that I believe contain the destiny of the U.S. solar industry. Let's quickly review.

1. Lack of history means the pioneers will decide.
2. Manageable control of the primary product is a must.
3. The importance of long-term, ethical cash flow.
4. Relying on government incentives is risky.
5. Quality of the product and the integrity of all support personnel are vital to a good future.

It is my opinion that we only have a single one of these correctly in place. I believe the quality of the product (equipment) is currently sufficient to produce a solar industry built on stability. Unfortunately, I am saddened by my true belief that all of the other ingredients do not show us that this industry is on a stable foundation (yet). The ship that is carrying this industry set sail during our "perfect storm" of approximately 6-8 years ago. Whether this ship, known as the U.S. solar industry, can endure the ingredients of this storm remains to be seen. If we are able to stabilize this ship before it goes down, a very worthwhile product will bring a tremendous benefit to many people for years to come. It is my firm belief that this will only be accomplished through a public awareness that is **much broader** than is currently the case.

This increased awareness is the overwhelming priority of this book. Now, it is up to all of you. I may have exposed you to these ingredients, but it is up to all of you, the public, to change them. If you or someone you know is considering obtaining solar products or maybe even a career in solar, please make yourself or them more aware. Investigate all the options. Look long-term. Do not simply follow the crowd. Use commonsense. Above all else, use your intuition and instinct. What truly feels right for you?

"Listen"

Final Note

For those of you interested in the specific story that I shared throughout chapter 8, I would like to expand on the progress of those issues since that chapter was written. Upon completion of the first draft manuscript of this book, I contacted the secretary to the City Manager of Woodland, California. My purpose was to provide an exclusive copy of this draft manuscript to the City Manager with her assistance. I had written a letter addressed to the manager and included it with the manuscript. I then coordinated a time and place to meet his secretary and give her the document to pass along to him.

During our brief meeting in which my son was also in attendance, I explained to her what this document represented and also provided her with a copy of the letter. She understood the importance and informed me that the manager was out of the office for a few days for personal reasons. I gave her my business card and asked her to send me a short e-mail upon his receipt of the package to confirm he had obtained it. As of yet, I have not received any e-mail from her. Although I cannot absolutely confirm he received my document, I am very confident he did. Here is an exact copy of the letter I included with the draft manuscript that was provided to his secretary. I have hidden his name intentionally.

To: XXXX   August 15, 2014
City Manager, Woodland California

Hello XXXX,

My name is Joe Gwerder. To my knowledge we have not met. I am a Yolo County native of 55 years. I have previously lived in Woodland for approximately 18 years. I now reside in Capay Valley. My professional roots are primarily as a General Contractor, although I have had several other businesses during my younger years also. For the past eight years or so I have mostly focused on solar design and installation. Over the years my companies have successfully completed many construction projects and solar installations within the city of Woodland. The collection of papers accompanying this note are actually a manuscript for a book I am in the process of publishing. This is something that I wish to provide to you in advance of the actual finished published book which I expect to be completed and available to the public in October of this year. The primary reason for your advanced "draft" copy is to give you a specific opportunity. Although I will not delay publication or remove any of the content you now possess, I may add a "last minute" section to the end of the book that would provide any relevant updated information should I deem it valuable.

This book, and specifically chapter 8, is extremely important to the reputation and operation of The City of Woodland Building Department. I wish to ask you to realize this is the main content only and not the actual finished copy I will send to my publisher during the week of August 18th to 22nd. This is my fourth book with this publisher, so we have a very familiar working relationship. I am very confident of a 6-8 week publishing timeframe. Also you will notice a few missing diagrams, graphs and pictures that have not been completed and inserted yet. These will have little impact on your understanding of the messages being delivered. Also missing is the back cover content and some of the supporting pages that will likewise have little effect on your grasp of the overall concept.

I wish to express to you that this is copyright material and you cannot reproduce or alter it. However, you may share it with those you deem necessary to address the issues exposed in chapter 8. Also, I encourage you to realize my intent of exposure. I am giving you an exclusive, limited time opportunity to learn of my experiences with The City of Woodland Building Department prior to this information becoming public. Once it is public however, I will continue increased exposure with my personal efforts in an array of arenas. The Woodland City

Council, various investigative reporters etc. Along with these methods I will periodically post self-created articles on my website. It saddens me that this situation came to be, but so important is its exposure for the purpose of change that I believe it was only a matter of time until you were faced with this realization, considering your job title. I do have one final request. Until you and I have established a mutual trustworthy relationship (if we eventually do), I ask that we only communicate in writing or verbally in a group setting. I do not wish to engage any private conversations with any City of Woodland employees concerning the matter exposed in chapter 8 until which time I believe I can actually trust any given particular individual. For your best opportunity to understand me and my priorities, I strongly suggest you read the entire manuscript in its proper sequence. Should you choose not to do this, then as mentioned before it is chapter 8 that is relevant to you.

Remember, another word for change is growth.

Thank you.

Joe Gwerder
Owner: Custom Design and Construction
Constant Energy Source

Author: Listen Without Your Ears
Listen Out Loud
20/20 Listening
Solar Integrity (coming in fall of 2014)

As you have seen, the letter was dated August 15, 2014. It is reasonable to assume that the document was in his possession within the following week based on his secretary's projection of his return to work. As we have progressed through the publishing process, I have waited to include this final note until the last window of opportunity was available to add this section to the book. My purpose for the delay was simply to allow as much time as I could for any feedback I might receive. It is mid-September as I write this and there has been no communication between the City Manager's office and myself.

I wish to make clear my intent with the exposure of the City of Woodland Building Department and their actions. I do not wish to dictate any particular or specific changes. I absolutely do wish to encourage those whose job it is to manage such affairs, to actually perform their duties in this matter. My personal purpose is to promote change toward an improved relationship between public employees and those in the community in which they serve. I do in fact hope that this exposure helps to accomplish such an improvement within this city, and on an even larger scale, I sincerely hope that an increased awareness is brought to city and county governments throughout our nation. At this point in my life, I do not wish to show up at City Council meetings and demand a change while pounding my fist on the podium.

My priority is to write. This is my greatest tool. It is through my writing that I reveal and expose. It is in this way that I can have the largest impact. By bringing awareness, I am performing the first step toward change. Encompassed within the second stage of acceptance and accountability is where many more people must become involved. Only when the individual leaders and managers in our public entities accept the responsibility of accountability, will actual changes occur.

I will end this book with an invitation to any of you who are interested, to frequent my website listed at the beginning of this book. Here you will find many articles I have written and additional information that I will continue to share. I can say with confidence that I will write additional books in the near future. Although I do not know for sure if any of these future books will address the subject of the solar industry, I suspect there will be such a book. I sincerely hope you have gained perspective and awareness through the information presented here.

The integrity of the solar industry in California and likely throughout the entire country is in desperate need of improvement in my opinion. I have presented all of this material in the best way I know in order to promote and easy-to-understand concept of how this industry functions at the consumer level. If you feel this book provides valuable information, please spread the word. The quicker more people are aware, the sooner positive changes will occur.

Thank you for your support and concern toward a very special interest. Of the three most common forms of natural clean energy sources that consist of solar, wind, and hydropower, there is really only one of them that is available on a private basis to millions of people. Although wind turbines and hydro generators are very good producers of power on a large scale, it is the flexibility and small configurations of solar power that makes it the most available clean power source to the public. Let's not allow the misguided intentions of a few screw up such a good potential.

A.C. (Alternating Current) – Typical power type required and recognized by public and private utilities in North America.

Array/Solar Array – An entire grouping of modules at a given location.

Back fed/Back feed – Power that is generated on location may be "back fed" into the utility grid. In this case the utility is receiving power from the generation location.

Cash Purchase – As the name implies, no form of financing used. Complete and direct payment transaction between the consumer and provider.

Circuit – A load or supply grouping of attached conductors, loads, outlets, switches, etc. Typically a certain wire and all that is connected to it from the power supply to all of the involved loads. A path of travel concerning a particular collection of loads and the conductor.

Current/Amps/Amperage – All synonymous in referring to electrical flow. Recognized as electricity volume of flow.

Conductor – Metal objects that allow the flow of current/amperage.

D.C. (Direct Current) – Type of power generated by the modules via sunlight. Not compatible with utility power in North America.

Disconnect/Disconnect Switch – A means to disengage electrical components. A quick and easy device used to interrupt the flow of current. Safety switch.

Ground/Bond – A means by which electricity can be absorbed into the earth. A conductive metal wire and/or rod to insure safety of all electrical components and anything that makes contact with them.

Inverter – Electrical appliance that transforms D.C. power to A.C. power.

Kilowatt – 1,000 watts, one thousand watts.

Kilowatt Hour (kWh) – Production or consumption of 1,000 watts (1 kilowatt) for a time of 1 total hour. Form of measurement typically used by utility companies. Not necessarily realized as 60 successive minutes, but rather a total of 60 minutes.

Main Panel – Electrical supply box in which utility service power is provided to a location. Point of contact between utility power supply and location load demands (requirements) and/or location generation equipment.

Megawatt – 1,000,000 watts, one million watts.

OCPD (Overcurrent Protection Device) – Typically referred to as a "breaker". An intentionally designed and installed weak point to provide protection from overheating circuits.

P.T.O. (Permission to Operate) – A term used by utility companies to announce their approval of the coexistence between a generation facility and the grid. Approval by the utility for the solar system to be turned on and attached to the grid.

P.V. (Photovoltaic) – Generating voltage from sunlight.

P.V. System Rated Size (A.C.) – The determination of a completely functional system after all expected losses are factored in. A much more realistic estimation of a systems production value based on the parameters of the location, equipment type, size, and arrangement, etc.

P.V. System Rated Size (D.C.) – The determination of a completely functional system prior to any losses due to location, voltage drop, or component arrangements. Calculated by simply multiplying the module rating by the total quantity of modules.

Parallel Wiring – Method of connecting multiple positive terminals or multiple negative terminals to a common D.C. component respectively. Purpose is to increase or multiply current/amperage.

R.O.I. (Return on Investment) – A period of time that is calculated to show an estimated "payback" timeframe. Length of time to recuperate ones investment.

Rack/Racking – Assortment of framework materials used to support the solar modules. Attached by various means to a roof structure or ground anchored structure.

Series Wiring – Method of connecting positive to negative output terminals on D.C. components. Purpose is to increase or multiply voltage.

Single Phase – Typical type of available or required power supply. Common in residential and small commercial locations. Provides for two current/amperage carrying conductors.

Solar Equipment Lease – Arrangement in which a third party other than the consumer or utility retain ownership of the equipment after it is installed at a location.

Solar Module (Module) – Typically referred to as a panel. One unit of solar cells typically housed in a rigid frame.

Standard Financed Equipment Purchase – Typically provided for commercial and/or agricultural operations and usually not restricted to any particular type of equipment.

String/Stringing – Refers to a group of modules wired in a series.

Subpanel – Additional load and/or supply electrical panel box placed on the consumer side of the utility main panel box. Typically used for additional space and/or supply multiple loads beyond the main panel. Also used as a power supply panel box for electrical attachments between solar inverter(s) and location loads and/or as a means to "back feed" power.

Three Phase – Large type of available or required power supply. Common in medium and large scale commercial and agricultural locations. Provides for three current/amperage carrying conductors.

Tier(s) – A term used to reference a level of cost and/or kWh allotment in a certain level of a utilities rate structure.

True-up Period/True-up – Indication of a timeframe in which produced and consumed power is exchanged with the utility. Typically 365 days of coexistence which then results in a balancing of payments. Produced and consumed (kWh's) kilowatt hours are tallied and summarized for the listed timeframe (typically 1 year) and a final payment is issued in either direction if the arrangement so states. A new time period is then started. The utility and consumer "true-up" at the end of each of the predetermined timeframes.

Volts/Voltage – A measurement of electrical pressure. Electrical force.

Watts/Wattage – End result of produced or consumed power. Form of measurement to determine total supply or needs. Volts × Amps = Watts

Wire – Typical metal conductor used to transport amperage from point "A" to point "B".